COUNTRIES OF THE WORLD

Denmark

Gareth Stevens Publishing
A WORLD ALMANAC EDUCATION GROUP COMPANY

About the Author: Clayton Trapp is a graduate of Louisiana State University, where he completed extensive studies on the life and work of Søren Kierkegaard, and the University of San Diego School of Law. He has worked as an author, editor, and journalist in the United States and Europe. Trapp's wife, Theresa, is of Danish descent.

Written by
CLAYTON TRAPP

Edited by
KATHARINE BROWN

Edited in the U.S. by
MONICA RAUSCH
PETER SCHMIDTKE

Designed by
LYNN CHIN

Picture research by
SUSAN JANE MANUEL

First published in North America in 2002 by
Gareth Stevens Publishing
A World Almanac Education Group Company
330 West Olive Street, Suite 100
Milwaukee, Wisconsin 53212 USA

Please visit our web site at:
www.garethstevens.com
For a free color catalog describing
Gareth Stevens Publishing's list of high-quality books
and multimedia programs, call 1-800-542-2595
or fax your request to (414) 332-3567.

© **TIMES MEDIA PRIVATE LIMITED 2002**
Originated and designed by
Times Editions
An imprint of Times Media Private Limited
A member of the Times Publishing Group
Times Centre, 1 New Industrial Road
Singapore 536196
http://www.timesone.com.sg/te

Library of Congress Cataloging-in-Publication Data
Trapp, Clayton.
    Denmark / Clayton Trapp.
        p. cm. — (Countries of the world)
Summary: Provides an overview of the geography, history, government, language, art, and food of Denmark.
    ISBN 0-8368-2350-8 (lib. bdg.)
    1. Denmark—Juvenile literature. [I. Denmark.]
    I. Title. II. Series.
    DL109.T75   2002
    948.9—dc21   2002023048

Printed in Malaysia

1 2 3 4 5 6 7 8 9 06 05 04 03 02

Contents

AN OVERVIEW OF DENMARK

The Kingdom of Denmark is located in northern Europe. Once the center of a great overseas empire, the Kingdom of Denmark today is made up of Denmark and the self-governing Faroe Islands and Greenland. A place of breathtaking beauty, Denmark's landscape is characterized by gently rolling hills, flat plains, and hundreds of islands.

Although it is a relatively small country, Denmark has strongly influenced the political and cultural development of other nations throughout the centuries. The country has a rich history filled with mighty Vikings and powerful kings. Denmark, however, is now a peaceful nation that has strong political and trade relations with its neighbors.

Opposite: **Built by King Christian IV in 1606, this magnificent Renaissance castle stands in the heart of Copenhagen, Denmark's capital city. The castle is now a museum, and its surrounding park is a favorite haven for city dwellers.**

Below: **Danes begin to enjoy bicycle rides at an early age.**

THE FLAG OF DENMARK

The flag of Denmark is known as the *Dannebrog* (DAY-nuh-broo), which means "Danish cloth." The flag consists of a white cross resting on a red background. The cross represents the country's Christian heritage. Originally, the lines that make up the cross were equal in length, but gradually the horizontal line became elongated. This design element of the Dannebrog was subsequently adopted by the other Nordic countries of Finland, Iceland, Norway, and Sweden. Legend has it that the Dannebrog fell from the sky to the Danish king Valdemar II on June 15, 1219, during his crusade to Estonia.

Geography

Located in northern Europe, Denmark lies immediately north of Germany. Water borders the country on three sides: the Skagerrak strait is to the north, the Kattegat and the Øresund straits lie to the east, and the North Sea is to the west. Denmark consists of the peninsula of Jutland and about five hundred islands. The Kingdom of Denmark also includes the Faroe Islands and Greenland, both of which are self-governing. Excluding these two territories, Denmark has an area of 16,639 square miles (43,094 square kilometers).

Jutland

Making up two-thirds of Denmark's land, the peninsula of Jutland is 100 miles (161 kilometers) wide at its broadest point and 200 miles (322 km) long. The lands of northern and eastern Jutland offer rich soil, which is the legacy of glaciers that once covered the area. Århus, located halfway down the eastern coast, is an important seaport and the country's second-largest city. A low range of hills in the eastern-central part of the peninsula includes the country's highest point, Yding Skovhøj, at 568 feet (173 meters).

GREENLAND

Located in the North Atlantic Ocean, Greenland is a self-governing part of the Kingdom of Denmark. The largest island in the world, Greenland is a land of glaciers, icebergs, reindeer, polar bears, seals, and whales and is home to the Inuit people (*above*).

(*A Closer Look, page 56*)

THE FAROE ISLANDS

The Faroe Islands (*left*) are located between Scotland's Shetland Islands and Iceland. With a total area of 540 square miles (1,399 square km), the Faroe Islands are made up of seventeen inhabited islands, one uninhabited island, and a few islets. The islands have been a self-governing part of the Kingdom of Denmark since 1948.

Stretching downward from the northern tip of the peninsula, the western coast of Jutland is formed by an almost unbroken belt of sand dunes. Swept by winds coming in from the Skagerrak, this area is sparsely populated. From Esbjerg to the German border, however, the region consists of well-tilled farms and conifer plantations.

The Islands

The Danish islands have rich, fertile soil that is ideal for farming. The islands are also similar in formation, with low hills, tiny lakes, and sandy beaches. Separated from Sweden by the Øresund, Zealand is the largest and most densely populated of Denmark's islands. Copenhagen, the country's capital city, is located on this island. Funen, the second-largest island, is located between Jutland and Zealand. The island of Bornholm lies in the Baltic Sea off the southern coast of Sweden. The foundation of the island is granite rather than the rich, softer soil that typifies other Danish islands. Other islands include Ærø, Falster, Langeland, Lolland, and Møn. Møn is renowned for the white chalk cliffs that rise to heights of over 400 feet (122 m) along its coasts.

Above: Copenhagen, Denmark's capital city, is an important center of commerce.

FJORDS AND WATERWAYS

Denmark has a coastline 4,545 miles (7,313 km) long, and its coasts are marked by small sea inlets, known as fjords. Limfjord, the largest of these inlets, separates northern Jutland from the rest of the peninsula. The Gudenå is the country's longest river. The river flows for 98 miles (158 km) before emptying into the Randers Fjord on the eastern coast of Jutland. With an area of 15.7 square miles (41 square km), Lake Arresø, on Zealand, is the country's largest lake.

Climate

Denmark enjoys a temperate climate, despite its northerly location. Temperatures are kept mild by the seas surrounding the country and prevailing western winds, the air of which is warmed by the Gulf Stream. Little fluctuation occurs between day and night temperatures, but changes in wind direction cause considerable changes in daily temperature.

Danish winters are wet, with long periods of frost, and temperatures fall to an average of 32° Fahrenheit (0° Celsius). During winter, freezing weather can last from 70 days on the western coast of Jutland to 120 days in the interior. Danish summers are mild, with temperatures reaching an average of 61° F (16° C). Day-to-day weather is changeable and can vary from cloudy to sunny.

Precipitation falls throughout the year, with the greatest rainfall occurring from late summer to early winter. The least amount of rain falls in February and April. While the Danish islands receive about 16 inches (41 centimeters) of rain a year, southwestern Jutland receives 32 inches (81 cm).

Above: Yellow fields of rape, a plant in the mustard family, brighten the countryside on Funen Island in early summer.

SUMMER SUNSHINE

During the months of June, July, and August, the days in Denmark are extremely long, especially in the country's northernmost areas. During these months, the Sun shines almost continuously within the Arctic Circle. Danish skies stay bright late into the night and brighten early in the morning.

Plants and Animals

Deciduous trees, including beech, oak, elm, and linden, abound in the forests that cover 10 percent of the country. Spruce and fir also thrive in Denmark, particularly in parts of Jutland where extensive areas of dune vegetation and heather have been reclaimed for forestry.

Many of Denmark's large mammals have died out, but roe deer still roam the countryside, and red deer make their homes in the forests of Jutland. Smaller animals, such as hares, foxes, squirrels, and hedgehogs, live throughout the country.

Denmark's bird life is more diverse. More than three hundred species of birds can be found in Denmark, of which about half breed in the nation. Storks once nested in large numbers in the marshes of Jutland at the beginning of the twentieth century. These birds have become rare because most of the peninsula's marshes have been drained to create farmland.

The country's fjords and surrounding seas provide excellent habitats for a wide array of marine life. Limfjord is home to oysters and mussels, while cod, herring, mackerel, shrimp, eels, and whitings are abundant in the North Sea.

Above: Red squirrels usually make their homes in coniferous or mixed woods. They eat tree seeds, such as hazelnuts and seeds from conifer cones, as well as tree flowers and shoots, mushrooms, and fungi from under tree bark.

NATIONAL BIRD

The peaceful, majestic, long-necked mute swan is the national bird of Denmark.

ALTERNATIVE FUELS

In recent years, Denmark has made considerable efforts to develop renewable energy sources, such as wind power.
(*A Closer Look, page 44*)

Left: Weighing up to 441 pounds (200 kilograms), the red deer is the largest wildlife species found in Denmark.

History

The first nomadic culture in Denmark developed around 12,000 B.C. By 4,000 B.C., inhabitants of the area had begun to farm and raise livestock. Between 500 B.C. and A.D. 400, a village society was established, and trade routes were developed with the peoples of the Mediterranean region.

Following years of strife between rival kings, Gorm became king of Jutland around 940 and, for the first time, unified present-day Denmark under one ruler. By the end of the tenth century, Christianity was the main religion in Denmark.

The Era of the Valdemars

From 1157 onward, Denmark became a prosperous nation under kings Valdemar I and Valdemar II. The economy flourished, and the country's territorial boundaries were expanded along the Baltic Sea. After Valdemar II's death in 1241, Denmark was plagued by a long period of civil war and conflict between the crown, church, and nobility. Valdemar IV reestablished the crown's power in 1340.

DANISH VIKINGS

Between the ninth and eleventh centuries, Danish Vikings sailed the waters of Europe, striking fear into their enemies. The three centuries during which the Vikings reigned changed Denmark forever. From being an almost unknown pagan area, the country developed into a well-defined kingdom, whose kings came to occupy the English throne.

(A Closer Look, page 50)

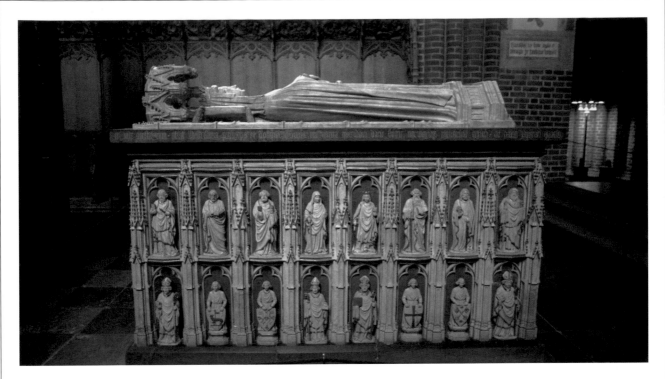

The Kalmar Union

In 1380, Denmark and Norway were joined in a union under Danish king Olaf. After his death in 1387, his mother, Margaret I, became regent of Denmark and Norway. Margaret's troops defeated Swedish king Albert in 1389, and, in 1397, her great-nephew Erik of Pomerania was crowned king of Denmark, Norway, and Sweden, marking the beginning of the Kalmar Union. Margaret, however, ruled as regent until her death in 1412.

Erik's subsequent rule antagonized the Swedish and Norwegian nobles, and he was eventually deposed in all three kingdoms in the union between 1438 and 1442.

From the Kalmar Union to the Reformation

Danish king Christian II's attempts to assert his authority in Sweden led to a Swedish uprising, which culminated in Sweden breaking away from the Kalmar Union in 1523. Denmark and Norway, however, remained united.

In 1534, civil war broke out in Denmark, and the forces of Prince Christian (later King Christian III) eventually prevailed in 1536. Christian then set about confiscating property and land from the Roman Catholic Church, paving the way for the Danish Reformation. In 1536, the Lutheran faith became the state religion.

Above: **Margaret I is entombed in the cathedral of Roskilde.**

VALDEMAR I

Following years of internal strife, Denmark emerged as a powerful and united nation under the rule of King Valdemar I, also known as Valdemar the Great.
(A Closer Look, page 72)

Opposite: **This is an illustration from the Ingeborg Psalter, which was a popular type of manuscript during the twelfth century.**

ACTS OF AGGRESSION

Although Denmark attempted to remain neutral after the outbreak of the Napoleonic Wars, efforts by Britain to blockade the European continent led to naval clashes. Much of the Danish fleet was destroyed during a battle with the British navy in the harbor of Copenhagen in 1801 (*left*). Denmark was forced to surrender the entire Danish fleet to Britain six years later.

Centuries of Warfare

Between 1543 and 1720, Denmark competed with Sweden for commercial and political control of the Baltic Sea and fought numerous military campaigns against Swedish forces. By 1660, Denmark had lost the territory it had controlled in southern Sweden, and the country was reduced to around one-third of its former size. Peace between Denmark and Sweden was finally established in 1720, when both countries, exhausted by nearly two hundred years of warfare, resolved their border disputes.

Peace, however, did not last. In 1807, Denmark became involved in the Napoleonic Wars. Denmark sided with France and Russia and remained an ally of France until 1814. After suffering defeat at the hands of Sweden, Denmark gave up its rights to Norway but still controlled the Norwegian colonies of Iceland, the Faroe Islands, and Greenland.

Social, Economic, and Political Changes

In 1849, Denmark adopted its first democratic constitution. The constitution guaranteed the civic rights of the people and gave power to an elected bicameral parliament.

The late 1800s saw social and political reforms in nearly all aspects of Danish life, including education, industry, and trade. Danish farmers developed cooperatives, and, by 1900, Danish workers had organized themselves into powerful labor unions

THE EIGHTY-SEVEN-YEAR PEACE

The period between 1720 and 1807 was the longest period of peace that Denmark had ever enjoyed up until the nineteenth century. During this time, the economy began to flourish as demands for agricultural products increased. This economic boom also created the basis for the country's prospering overseas trade and shipping. In addition, a national identity was born as Danes began to identify themselves with their nation, language, and history.

Opposite: These Danish women celebrate the liberation of Denmark by Allied forces on May 5, 1945.

that were able to demand higher wages for workers. In 1915, a new constitution abolished the special rights of the upper classes and granted women the right to vote. The Danish economy was also strong during this period, and the Danish merchant navy grew into one of the largest fleets of trading ships in the world.

Denmark and the Two World Wars

Denmark declared its neutrality when World War I broke out in 1914 and sought to protect its economic interests. After the war, however, economic conditions deteriorated, and unemployment soared. In an attempt to promote its nonaggressive policy, Denmark joined the League of Nations, an international alliance established to peacefully settle disputes between nations, in 1920.

While the Danish government introduced measures to improve social conditions within the country during the 1930s, Denmark's foreign policy was dominated by its relationship with Germany. Concerned about Germany's rearmament program, Denmark signed a nonaggression treaty with its neighbor in 1939. Although Denmark declared its neutrality at the outbreak of World War II, German troops invaded the country on April 9, 1940, and occupied the nation until May 5, 1945.

DENMARK AND ICELAND

Iceland came under Danish rule when Norway and Denmark united in 1380. The country became an independent state in 1918 and became known as the Republic of Iceland in 1944, after cutting all ties with Denmark.

DENMARK AND THE HOLOCAUST

During the Nazi occupation of Denmark between 1940 and 1945, the Danish population became increasingly active in a resistance movement that carried out acts of sabotage against the Germans and helped save over 95 percent of the nation's Jewish population.

(A Closer Look, page 54)

Postwar History

After the end of World War II, Denmark joined international organizations that dealt with the collective defense of Western powers. In addition, successive socialist governments attempted to strengthen the economy. In 1968, a coalition of non-socialist parties was elected to power, marking the end of four decades of political domination by the Social Democratic Party.

By the mid-1970s, Denmark was plagued by economic difficulties, following the 1974–1975 world economic slump. Since then, successive governments have focused their attention on economic issues, such as unemployment and inflation.

In 1972, Denmark voted to become a member of the European Economic Community (EEC), now known as the European Union (EU). The country's subsequent relationship with the union has been strained at times, particularly over social and environmental issues. The Danish population as a whole is wary of the effects of increased political and monetary integration with the rest of Europe. In September 2000, Denmark voted against a bid to change its currency to the euro, the EU's common currency.

Below: A member of the Social Democratic Party, Poul Nyrup Rasmussen was Denmark's prime minister from 1993 to 2001.

King Christian IV (1577–1648)

King Christian IV ruled Denmark and Norway from 1588 to 1648. During his reign, trade and shipping flourished, and he also built many beautiful buildings and established new cities. Christian's main concern in foreign policy was the threat of Swedish expansion into the Baltic region, and, against the advice of his councillors, he entered the Thirty Years' War in Germany in 1624. The defeat of his forces in 1626 marked the beginning of the gradual decline of Denmark-Norway's role in European politics. Although Christian's foreign policies weakened the kingdom's economy, he is generally regarded as one of the greatest Danish rulers.

King Christian IV

Queen Margaret I (1353–1412)

A highly skilled monarch and diplomat, Margaret I became the undisputed ruler of Denmark, Norway, and Sweden in 1397. Born in 1353, Margaret married Haakon VI, king of Norway, ten years later. With the death of her father in 1375, Margaret secured the Danish throne for her son, Olaf; she also ruled Norway after the death of Haakon in 1380. When Olaf died in 1387, Margaret became regent of both Norway and Denmark. In 1389, her forces defeated the Swedish king, paving the way for the Kalmar Union in 1397. Uniting Denmark, Norway, and Sweden under a strong monarch, Margaret ruled the union until her death in 1412. During her reign, Margaret skillfully centralized power and established peace throughout the kingdom.

Queen Margaret I

Thorvald Stauning (1873–1942)

Elected secretary of the Social Democratic Party in 1898, Thomas Stauning became a member of the *Folketing* (FULL-guh-ting) in 1906. Stauning was elected prime minister in 1924 but was defeated in the 1926 elections because the monetary reforms of his government worsened conditions in industry and agriculture. Stauning served again as prime minister between 1929 and 1942. During this period, he introduced important economic and social welfare legislation. Although German forces occupied Denmark in 1940, Stauning continued to lead a coalition government until his death in 1942.

Thorvald Stauning

Government and the Economy

Denmark is a constitutional monarchy. The current constitution, which was adopted in 1953, abolished the upper house of parliament and allowed the succession of women to the throne.

Denmark's government is made up of legislative, executive, and judicial branches. Legislative power is vested jointly in the sovereign, or monarch, and a unicameral parliament, called the Folketing. The Folketing is made up of 179 members, including two from Greenland and two from the Faroe Islands. Danish voters elect 135 members of the Folketing to four-year terms by voting for political parties in their local constituencies. The remaining forty seats are divided among the parties, based on each party's proportion of the nationwide vote.

Although appointed by the sovereign, the prime minister must have the support of the majority of the Folketing. About twenty additional ministers run government departments, such as justice, finance, and agriculture, and collectively make up the

THE MONARCHY

Highly respected by the Danish population, the country's monarch, Queen Margrethe II (*above*), succeeded to the throne in 1972.
(*A Closer Look*, page 62)

cabinet. The current prime minister, Anders Fogh Rasmussen, was voted into office in 2001. The sovereign, Queen Margrethe II, is the chief of state, but her duties are primarily ceremonial.

Denmark's judiciary is independent of the executive and legislative branches. The country has three levels of courts: city courts, High Courts, and the Supreme Court. City courts handle most cases. The two High Courts hear appeals from the city courts and handle serious criminal cases, which are heard by a judge and a jury of twelve people. The Supreme Court is the highest court in the land and consists of fifteen judges who are appointed for life by the sovereign on the recommendation of the government.

Local Government

Denmark is divided into fourteen counties. Each county is governed by a county council that is elected every four years. The county council then chooses its own chairman, or county mayor. The councils' primary responsibilities include road building and maintenance, health and hospital services, and general education.

Above: **Former prime minister Poul Nyrup Rasmussen addresses members of the Folketing in 2000.**

Opposite: **Built between 1892 and 1905, Copenhagen Town Hall was designed by architect Martin Nyrop.**

ARMED FORCES

National service is compulsory for Danish men. All young men must register at the age of eighteen and are subject to at least nine months of military training in the army, the navy, or the air force. Women can volunteer for service, including service on combat vessels.

Economy

Denmark is traditionally an agricultural nation. In recent years, however, the manufacturing sector has increased in importance and now contributes more to national income than agriculture. Today, the economy is based primarily on service industries, manufacturing, and trade.

During the second half of the twentieth century, the number of people working in agriculture decreased dramatically, while employment in public and private service industries soared. Today, 79 percent of the Danish workforce is employed in the services sector, which includes education and health care.

Manufacturing has greatly expanded since the end of World War II and now employs 17 percent of the workforce. The construction, food-processing, machinery, clothing, and textile industries are extremely important to the Danish economy.

Although almost two-thirds of Denmark's total land area is under cultivation, agriculture only employs 4 percent of the workforce. Most of the cultivated land is in Jutland, and the majority of farms are small- and medium-sized. More than half

Above: **This man is packing relief supplies for the United Nations Children's Fund (UNICEF) in a factory in Copenhagen.**

of the cultivated land is used to grow cereals, including barley and wheat. Important tuber crops are potatoes, sugar beets, and turnips. Livestock is also important to Denmark's agricultural economy, and Danes raise dairy cattle, pigs, and poultry. Due to intensive mechanization and the widespread use of fertilizers, Danish farms produce high yields.

The country's long coastline provides Danish fishermen with excellent fishing grounds. The most important catches include cod, herring, and plaice. Fishing is an important source of domestic food supply. In addition, both fresh and processed fish are important exports.

Denmark's natural resources are limited. Therefore, the country imports raw materials, animal feed, and fertilizers to meet its needs. The nation, however, produces enough oil and gas to satisfy its own energy requirements and leads the world in energy conservation and the development of energy products such as windmills and heating controls. Kaolin is found on the island of Bornholm, but its quality is poor. Other minerals produced commercially are limonite, lignite, limestone, and chalk.

The country's main export and import trading partners are other members of the EU, Norway, and the United States.

OVERFISHING

Extensive fishing by Danish fishermen has led to overfishing and a subsequent shortage of fish. This environmental dilemma has been further complicated by the fact that Denmark ranks among the top ten fishing nations in the world in terms of the value of its catch.
(A Closer Look, page 64)

TRANSPORTATION

Denmark has an excellent transportation system, including roads, railways, ferries, and airplanes. More than half of the population, however, uses bicycles for transportation, and most roads have separate bicycle lanes. Copenhagen is the transportation hub of the country, with the largest seaport and Kastrup Airport. Along with Sweden and Norway, Denmark owns Scandinavian Airlines (SAS), which flies all over the world. The government-owned railroad provides efficient passenger services to cities and towns. Ferries connect the Danish islands with the mainland, as well as with each other.

Left: Officially opened on July 1, 2000, the Øresund Bridge links Copenhagen, Denmark's capital city, to Malmö in Sweden.

People and Lifestyle

The population of the Kingdom of Denmark consists of Danish, Inuit, and Faroese peoples. Denmark is almost entirely inhabited by Danes, who are of indigenous northern European stock and among the most homogeneous peoples of Europe. Most Faroese are descended from the Vikings who settled on the islands in the ninth century, while Greenlanders are Inuit or of mixed Inuit and European origin. Denmark also has a small German minority in southern Jutland.

The Danish culture is warm and friendly, and all ethnic groups receive respect. A central concept of Danish culture is *hygge* (HOO-guh), which loosely translates as "cozy and snug." The term suggests shutting out the trials and tribulations of the outside world and opting for personal warmth and intimacy.

Although immigration is limited, people from other nations, such as Turkey, have come to Denmark to work as guest workers. The 1980s and 1990s brought new waves of immigrants from Iraq, Somalia, the former Yugoslavia, Iran, and Afghanistan.

IT IS ALL IN THE NAME

Approximately two-thirds of the Danish population have surnames that end in "sen," such as Jensen and Hansen. Until the end of the nineteenth century, "sen" was added to the end of the father's first name to denote the surname of the child. Therefore, if a child was named James and was the son of Peder Andersen, he would be known as James Pedersen. A daughter took the surname of her father.

City and Rural Life

Denmark is a highly urbanized nation, with about 86 percent of the population living in urban areas. Slightly more than one-quarter of the population lives in the greater Copenhagen area. Other populous cities include Århus, Odense, and Ålborg. With its extensive system of social services, Denmark has one of the highest standards of living in the world.

Most city dwellers live in apartments, while small houses dominate the suburbs. Those who wish to get away from city life often own or rent small plots of land outside the cities, on which they build small summerhouses or simply grow flowers, fruits, and vegetables.

Although Denmark's rural population has steadily decreased as more people move to the country's large cities, carefully tended farms still dot the countryside. Most Danish farms are small and run by the people who live on them. Rural residences have modern facilities, such as central heating, telephones, and refrigeration. Roofs of farmhouses are either thatched or made of red or blue tiles.

Above: **Danes pride themselves on being modern and casual. This young couple is enjoying a stroll down one of Copenhagen's main streets.**

Opposite: **Many Danes, such as these girls in Jutland, have blond hair and blue eyes.**

Above: **A Danish wedding is full of traditions, including the custom of riding in a horse-drawn carriage after the ceremony.**

Family Life

Danish family life revolves around the nuclear family. Families tend to be close-knit and are small, with a couple having one or two children. Sometimes extended family members also live under the same roof, but this situation is rare. Families spend a lot of time together, and family members gather to celebrate holidays and special occasions, such as baptisms, confirmations, and weddings. Such occasions include banquets and many speeches.

Today, most men and women work outside the home. Consequently, family members share household responsibilities. Danish children are brought up to be well mannered, responsible, and independent. Teenagers often have close and confidential relationships with their parents, and Danish children usually live with their parents until they reach their mid-twenties.

In Denmark, it is generally considered acceptable for couples to live together before marriage, and most couples do so. In addition, many Danish families are "paperless," whereby couples live together but do not go through the formalities of marriage. In recent years, the number of divorces has increased, and single-parent families are becoming more common.

Women in Denmark

Today, Danish women lead independent lives, and they have been entering universities and the professions in increasing numbers in recent years. Women make up about half the Danish workforce, and most women continue working after marriage. They work in all sectors, including the armed forces, but they are still underrepresented in senior business positions. Although the Equal Pay Act was passed in 1973, women continue to earn less than their male counterparts.

The government recognizes the important contributions that women make to the economy and has established kindergartens and other childcare centers to encourage women to work outside the home. Legislation has also been passed to ensure that employers provide twenty-four weeks of paid maternity leave.

Women are increasingly well represented at all levels of government, and currently five out of eighteen ministers in the cabinet are female. In addition, women's rights groups exist throughout the country and lobby the government in areas of concern, including wage inequality and parental leave.

THE DANISH WELFARE STATE

With the support of high taxes, the Danish government provides extensive social services, including free medical care, hospitalization, and some dental services. As a result of this outstanding welfare system, the life expectancy for Danes is very high. (*A Closer Look, page 52*)

Below: **More and more Danish women work in the services sector and play key roles in organizing large conferences such as this one in the concert hall of Tivoli Gardens in Copenhagen.**

Education

All Danes between the ages of seven and sixteen must attend school. Public schools are free, and parents have the right to choose which school their children attend. About 88 percent of Danish children attend public schools. The remainder go to private schools, which receive between 80 and 85 percent of their funding from the government.

Preschool and kindergarten education are optional, but many Danish children attend preschool or kindergarten classes between the ages of five and six. Students begin *folkeskole* (FULL-guh-skool), or elementary and middle school, at the age of seven. Subjects include Danish, mathematics, history, religion, science, and geography. English is compulsory from grade five onward. Additional subjects are added in the middle school grades.

Education beyond grade nine is voluntary but is open to all. Most students choose to continue their studies. About 41 percent attend vocational schools, while 53 percent opt to go to academic high schools. Vocational education includes specialized programs at commercial or technical schools and apprenticeships.

Below: **These children attend kindergarten in the city of Ålborg in northern Jutland.**

24

High school, or *gymnasium* (gim-NAY-shee-yoom), lasts for three years and aims to prepare students for higher education. Students can study numerous subject combinations, in addition to science/mathematics and language streams. At the end of the third year, students take the Upper Secondary School Leaving Examination, the results of which determine whether they can attend a university or a higher education institution. Young people and adults who have left the education system and wish to return to continue their studies can qualify for higher education by taking a two-year course of study that leads to the higher preparatory examination.

Higher Education

Denmark has five multifaculty universities, the oldest of which is the University of Copenhagen, founded in 1479. The country also has ten universities that specialize in fields such as engineering, veterinary science, art, architecture, and music.

Folk High Schools

An outstanding feature of Danish education is the system of folk high schools. These schools are residential institutions that offer courses in general subjects to adults. The schools are privately run but are supported financially by the government. Today, the country has about ninety-four folk schools, most of which offer courses in literature, music, drama, and social studies.

Religion

The Evangelical Lutheran Church is the established church of Denmark and replaced Roman Catholicism as the official religion after the Protestant Reformation in the sixteenth century. Today, about 95 percent of the Danish population is Evangelical Lutheran. Regular attendance at church services, however, is extremely low, at an estimated 5 percent.

Most Danes attend church at Christmas and Easter and for major life events, such as weddings and baptisms. Generally, the Danish people have a relaxed attitude toward the church, but the church has not lost its place in people's consciousness.

The Evangelical Lutheran Church is headed by the monarch, who is required by law to be a member of the church. The church is supported by the state through a special tax payable by all citizens who have not formally withdrawn from the church. The Folketing is the legislative authority of the church, while the supreme administrative body of the church is the Ministry of Ecclesiastical Affairs.

Above: **Also known as Frederikskirke, the Marble Church in Copenhagen was inspired by St. Peter's Church in Rome, Italy. Today, the church's copper dome is one of the most dominant features of the city's skyline.**

Denmark is divided into twelve dioceses, including those of Greenland and the Faroe Islands. Within each diocese, the bishop is the highest authority in spiritual matters and supervises the lower members of the clergy.

Other Faiths

Apart from Evangelical Lutheranism, other Protestant denominations include the Danish Baptist Church, the Seventh Day Adventists, the Methodist Church, and the Anglican Church. Religious communities of Jehovah's Witnesses and Mormons are also located throughout the country. Roman Catholicism is the second largest religion in Denmark, with about thirty-three thousand members. Other religions include Judaism, Hinduism, and Islam.

Folklore

Denmark was the first Nordic country to adopt Christianity as its official religion under King Harold in the tenth century. Before then, the Norse gods of the Vikings, including Thor, Odin, and Frey, and pagan rituals dominated spiritual beliefs and practices in Denmark.

SØREN KIERKEGAARD

Denmark's most famous philosopher, Søren Kierkegaard (1813–1855) is considered the father of existentialism. His works have had a great impact on both twentieth-century religious and secular thought.
(A Closer Look, page 58)

Below: **Many Danish churches, such as this one in the city of Ribe, have high, arched ceilings.**

Language and Literature

Danish is the official language of Denmark. Danish is closely related to Norwegian, Swedish, and Icelandic, all of which belong to the Scandinavian branch of the Germanic languages. The people of Greenland speak Greenlandic, a non-European language, while the people of the Faroe Islands speak Faroese. Faroese is distantly related to Danish. Denmark also has a small German-speaking minority in the southern part of Jutland. English, which is taught at school in Denmark, is the predominant second language.

Danish has two cases (nominative and genitive) and two noun genders (common and neuter). The definite article in Danish has two forms: one is placed before adjectives, while the other is placed at the end of nouns without adjectives. In addition, the Danish alphabet has three more letters than the English alphabet: æ, ø, and å.

HANS CHRISTIAN ANDERSEN

Author of stories such as *The Princess and the Pea* (1835), *The Ugly Duckling* (1844), and *The Emperor's New Clothes* (1837), Hans Christian Andersen (1805–1875) is world famous for his fairy tales.
(*A Closer Look, page 47*)

Below: A wide variety of newspapers is sold throughout Denmark, and Danes enjoy freedom of the press.

DENMARK'S NATIONAL POET

Denmark's national poet is dramatist and poet Adam Gottlob Oehlenschläger (1779–1850). He broke with eighteenth-century Danish literary traditions and introduced romanticism in his poem *Guldhornene* (1802), or *The Golden Horns*.

Literature

Literature plays an important part in Danish life, and many of the country's writers are known throughout the world. Ludvig Holberg (1684–1754) is widely acknowledged as the father of Danish literature, as well as the country's greatest classical writer. His brilliant comic poems and plays are known internationally. Hans Christian Andersen and the influential philosopher and religious thinker Søren Kierkegaard are the two most celebrated nineteenth-century Danish writers.

Many popular writers emerged in the early twentieth century, including Martin Andersen Nexø (1869–1954) and Tom Kristensen (1893–1974). Danish writers Karl Adolph Gjellerup (1857–1919) and Henrik Pontoppidan (1857–1943) shared the Nobel Prize for Literature in 1917. Another Danish author, Johannes Vilhelm Jensen (1873–1950), was awarded the same prize in 1944 for his series of novels that includes *Den lange rejse* (1908–1922; *The Long Journey*). Contemporary Danish writers include poet Marianne Larsen (1942–); Vita Andersen (1944–), whose works focus on the rise of feminism in Denmark; Klaus Rifbjerg (1931–); and Peter Høeg (1957–).

ISAK DINESEN

Born in 1885, Karen Blixen moved to Kenya with her husband in 1914. She divorced him in 1921 and returned to Denmark in 1931. Under the pseudonym Isak Dinesen, she wrote *Seven Gothic Tales* (1934), which dealt with the world of the supernatural. Three years later, Dinesen wrote the memoirs of her life in Kenya in the world-famous book *Out of Africa*. Her only novel, *The Angelic Avengers* (1944), was regarded by Danish readers as a clever satire of Nazi-occupied Denmark. Blixen died in 1962.

Arts

Music

Carl August Nielsen (1865–1931) is Denmark's most important composer. He wrote six symphonies, three concerti, two operas, and numerous chamber, choral, and keyboard works. His innovative compositions, which bridged romanticism and modernism, have inspired subsequent Danish composers, including Herman Koppel (1908–1998) and Ib Nørholm (1931–).

Distinguished Danish singers include tenor Lauritz Melchoir (1890–1973) and soprano Inga Nielsen (1946–). Victor Borge (1909–2000), also known as the "Great Dane," delighted audiences with his unique blend of comedy and classical music.

Traditional folk music is popular in Denmark. Today, favorite Danish folk musicians combine instruments and musical concepts from around the world with traditional Danish instrumental and vocal genres. In the world of pop and rock music, well-known Danish bands include Aqua, Michael Learns to Rock, and Kashmir.

COPENH

Below: Located at Langelinje Pier in Copenhagen, this bronze statue of the *Little Mermaid* was inspired by Hans Christian Andersen's fairy tale *The Little Mermaid* (1837). Sculpted by Edvard Eriksen (1876–1959), the statue sits on a large, granite stone overlooking the city's harbor. Today, this statue is a famous Danish landmark.

Sculpture and Painting

Denmark has produced many prominent sculptors and painters. Bertel Thorvaldsen (1770–1844) is the greatest sculptor to have come out of Denmark. A leader in the neoclassical movement, Thorvaldsen based his style on the traditions of the classical Mediterranean civilizations. He sculpted most of his works in white marble. The twentieth-century iron sculptures of Robert Jacobsen (1912–1993) have also won worldwide acclaim.

Until the 1800s, Danish art centered around formal portraits. The move away from this type of painting came with Christoffer Wilhelm Eckersberg (1783–1853), who portrayed scenes of everyday Danish life. Painters who based themselves at Skagen promoted marine painting and were the pioneers of Danish naturalism and neoromanticism. Popular Skagen painters included P. S. Kroyer (1851–1909) and Anna Ancher (1859–1935). Asger Jorn (1914–1973) was one of the most important Danish artists of the postwar period. He achieved international recognition for his abstract paintings.

Theater, Opera, and Dance

Danish theater, opera, and dance are of a high caliber. Today, Danish theater performs international works as well as classical and contemporary Danish plays. Opened in 1748, the Royal Theater is at the heart of the country's cultural life, and the Danish royal theater, opera, and ballet companies all perform here.

Danish opera thrives in Denmark and is becoming increasingly international through guest appearances and exchanges of well-known overseas opera stars. In addition, the establishment of Den Anden Opera, or the Other Opera, in 1994 has been of major importance to contemporary Danish opera and music drama.

Ballet has long been Denmark's most highly respected cultural field. Modern dance has finally made its mark in Denmark through the works of Byt Dansk Danseteater, or the New Danish Dance Theater. Interest in dance has also been fostered by events such as Dancin' City that bring the latest international dance styles to Copenhagen.

Above: **Located in Odense, Den Fynske Landsby, an open-air museum, presents a play based on one of the well-loved fairy tales of Denmark's Hans Christian Andersen.**

ROYAL DANISH BALLET

Since its establishment in the eighteenth century, the Royal Danish Ballet has become internationally famous. Today, the ballet company continues to perform classical dances as well as contemporary ballets.
(A Closer Look, page 68)

Crafts

Denmark is famous for beautifully designed ceramics, porcelain, silverware, and home furnishings, all of which emphasize simple elegance and functionality. Danish silverware is admired in both Denmark and abroad; the silver jewelry of Georg Jensen Silversmiths is highly prized and continues to adapt and change with the times. Denmark's exquisite porcelain has evolved to represent the high quality of all Danish crafts. Royal Copenhagen is noted for its excellent artistry and craftsmanship in both design and decoration.

Architecture

General European trends have dominated Danish architecture throughout the centuries. In the twentieth century, architecture was influenced by modernism. Distinguished architects include Arne Jacobsen (1902–1971), whose buildings are simple in design and use large expanses of glass, and Jørn Utzon (1918–), whose most famous design is the sail-like structure of the Sydney Opera House in Australia.

FLORA DANICA

One of the world's most famous sets of porcelain is the Flora Danica dinner service made by Royal Copenhagen (originally known as the Royal Copenhagen Porcelain Manufactory). The dinner service is regarded as one of the most original and inspired products to emerge from the golden age of porcelain. Commissioned by Crown Prince Frederik in 1790, the set took twelve years to complete. Each of the 1,802 pieces was hand-molded and hand-painted with a different native Danish wildflower or other plant and rimmed with gold. Of the original 1,802 pieces, 1,530 still exist today.

DESIGN

Modern Danish design stresses functional refinement of style and comfort. Hans J. Wegner (1914–) is world renowned for blending a variety of natural materials into his classic designs. The Egg Chair (*left*), designed by architect Arne Jacobsen, with its smooth curving lines, became an instant classic and a model for furniture designers. His Ant Chair became the model for the stacking chair found worldwide.

Leisure and Festivals

Danes enjoy social activities that involve their families and friends. Most Danish people split their leisure time between activities that exercise their bodies and pursuits that enhance their minds.

The Great Outdoors

Danes love the outdoors, and the country's endless nature trails provide many opportunities for outdoor enthusiasts to explore the countryside. Walking is a particularly popular pastime, and families often go for walks on weekends. The country has a network of walking paths, and walking associations often organize group walks.

Due to its relative flatness, Denmark is also ideal for cycling. Cycling paths with spectacular views are widespread throughout the countryside, and many of the country's roads have parallel bicycle tracks. Other popular outdoor pursuits are hunting, fishing, and visiting the country's sandy beaches.

LEGOLAND

Zebra-striped cars, fire-breathing dragons, and miniature replicas of international sights and well-known personalities — all of which are made entirely of Lego bricks — make up Legoland, Denmark's world-famous family attraction.
(A Closer Look, page 60)

Left: **Most Danish cities, such as Copenhagen, and towns have elaborate bicycle path systems.**

MUSEUMS

Denmark is home to hundreds of museums that are visited frequently by Danes. Copenhagen's National Museum has an extensive collection of Danish artifacts, which date back ten thousand years. Paintings and sculptures by Danish and European masters can be seen at the State Museum of Art, while more classically inclined art lovers visit the ancient Egyptian, Greek, and Roman exhibits at the Ny Carlsberg Glyptotek. The Louisiana Museum of Modern Art, located south of Helsingør, has one of the most celebrated collections of modern art.

Parks

Denmark is home to many beautiful parks, as well as a number of amusement and theme parks, including the world-famous Tivoli Gardens. Opened in 1843, Tivoli Gardens offers something for people of all ages, including rides, shooting galleries, circus acts and pantomime, restaurants, firework displays, theatrical performances, and beautiful gardens. In addition, dozens of castles, palaces, mansions, and manor houses, which are often set in age-old parks and gardens, are open to the public.

Indoor Activities

Since a commercial channel was introduced in 1988 and with the growing popularity and availability of cable television, Danes have started to watch more television. The Danish people also enjoy playing chess. Bent Larsen (1935–) is one of several Danish chess prodigies. Larsen became a grand master at the age of twenty-one and has won several international tournaments. Bridge and other card games are also popular.

Denmark is a nation of avid readers. About eighty-four million books are borrowed from the country's public libraries each year.

ROSKILDE FESTIVAL

Attracting big names over the years, such as Bob Marley and the Wailers, U2, Pearl Jam, and Robbie Williams, Roskilde Festival has developed from a local event to an international world-class music festival. Today, Roskilde boasts that it holds the best music festival in the world.

(*A Closer Look*, page 66)

Sports

Danes love sports and spend much of their leisure time participating in or watching one of the many sports they enjoy. The government actively promotes the importance of athletics, and local sports facilities, such as outdoor playing fields and track and field stadiums, are available throughout the country. Despite its relatively small size, Denmark excels in many sports and has produced a number of successful athletes.

About two-thirds of Danish children participate in organized sports. Favorite sports among boys include *fodbold* (FULL-buhn), or soccer; handball; and badminton, while girls prefer gymnastics, horseback riding, handball, and swimming.

Soccer is the most popular sport in Denmark, and the game is played at local, regional, and national levels. The country's top twelve soccer teams, including Brøndby, AGF Aarhus, and OB Odense, compete in the country's Faxe Kondi Liga, or premier league. Denmark has also established itself as a force on the international soccer scene and won the European Championship in 1992. In recent years, the national team has often ranked among the top twenty teams in the world.

GREAT SPORTING DANES

In 2000, Danish sportspeople won thirteen world championships in seven different sports. Famous soccer players include strikers Michael and Brian Laudrup and goalkeepers Peter Schmeichel and Thomas Sørensen. Mountain bike champion Michael Rasmussen was at the peak of his discipline in 1999, and cyclist Bjarne Ris won the Tour de France in 1996. Female Danish stars include handball player Anja Andersen and badminton player Camilla Martin.

Another popular sport in Denmark is speedway racing, in which motorcycles race around small, oval tracks. Denmark led the sport until the mid-1990s and has produced many first-class riders. Dane Hans Nielsen dominated the sport in the late 1980s and early 1990s.

Danes are well known for their athletic skills in gymnastics, swimming, tennis, and especially handball. The country's national female handball team won the gold medal in the 1996 and 2000 Olympic Games, as well as the world championship in 1997. Denmark also performs well in badminton, with Poul Erik Høyer winning the Olympic gold in 1996 and Camilla Martin becoming the world champion in 1999.

Water Sports

Denmark has a long coastline, many inland lakes and rivers, and a mild climate. All of these factors have helped Danes excel at water sports. Popular water sports include sailing, rowing, swimming, diving, wind surfing, and canoeing. Many Danes sail in their leisure time, and yachting is by far the country's most successful sport. One of Denmark's best-known and most successful sports personalities of all time is yachtsman Paul Elvstrøm, who won four successive Olympic gold medals in 1948, 1952, 1956, and 1960.

Festivals

The main festival of the year in Denmark is Christmas. Although many long-standing traditions have disappeared over the years, the custom of the family gathering at Christmas is still preserved.

The Monday before Ash Wednesday is called *Fastelavn* (fes-tuh-LAH-on). In earlier times, it was a period of fasting, but today the festival is marked by fun and games. Fastelavn is a school holiday, and parents are awakened by their children waving birch branches that have been specially decorated with paper and candy. Later, the children dress up in traditional costumes and go from door to door, asking their neighbors for candy or money.

Easter starts at the end of Lent on a Wednesday evening and runs from Maundy Thursday through Easter Monday. Common Prayer Day, the fourth Friday after Easter, is a public holiday.

Queen Margrethe II's birthday is celebrated on April 16. On this day, many children watch the parade of the royal guard at Amalienborg Square in Copenhagen and gather in front of the royal palace to wave small Danish flags.

Midsummer's Eve, on June 23, is a popular festival. On this night, people gather around bonfires, make speeches, and sing songs. A witch made of wood and cloth is placed on top of the bonfire to symbolize the burning of witches many centuries ago.

CHRISTMAS

Probably the most important holiday in Denmark, Christmas is celebrated with fervor throughout the country. Festivities start at the beginning of December and reach their climax on December 24 and 25.
(A Closer Look, page 48)

Left: **Danish families gather around a bonfire in Copenhagen to celebrate Midsummer's Eve.**

Liberation Day on May 5 is a national holiday that commemorates Denmark's liberation from the Nazis at the end of World War II. The observance begins on Liberation Eve when households display candles in their windows, as they did in anticipation of the arrival of the Allied forces in 1945.

Denmark also celebrates two half-day holidays on May 1 and June 5. May 1 is Worker's Day, and Danes often gather in parks or other public places to listen to speeches by politicians or other well-known personalities. Constitution Day on June 5 honors the day in 1849 when King Frederik VII signed the country's first constitution.

Denmark holds the largest celebrations outside the United States for American Independence Day on July 4. On this day, Americans of Danish descent are invited to homecoming festivities that include concerts, rallies, and lectures. Thousands attend this event every year.

The Danes also place special emphasis on the birthdays that mark each decade of a person's life. A person's sixtieth birthday is considered a particularly important occasion and is celebrated by a gathering of relatives and friends.

Above: **Each year on May 5, parades are held throughout Denmark to mark Liberation Day.**

MUSIC FESTIVALS

Throughout the year, Denmark hosts an array of musical events that include jazz, rock, blues, gospel, classical, and country music. The Copenhagen Jazz Festival is one of the world's major jazz festivals, while the Copenhagen Summer Festival features chamber and classical music concerts. Taking place during the first week of September, the Århus Festival offers opera and classical music as well as rock music and street performances.

Food

Danish food includes a wide variety of fish, meat, bread, cheese, and crispbreads. The Danes place great emphasis on arranging their food so it is visually attractive as well as tasty. Most Danes eat four meals a day: breakfast, lunch, dinner, and a late supper.

Breakfast usually consists of cereal and *morgenbrød* (MWARN-brohd), or bread and various types of rolls, served with cheese, jam, and sometimes eggs. *Smørrebrød* (SMUHR-brohd), an open-faced sandwich, is popular among Danes for lunch and for their late-evening suppers. Dinner is the main meal and is usually the only hot meal of the day.

The most traditional Danish dish is roast duckling stuffed with apples and prunes and served with red cabbage and boiled potatoes. Other favorites include *frikadeller* (FREY-guh-DIL-luh), or meatballs; *flæskesteg* (FLIE-skuh-tig), or roast pork with crackling; beer and potato stew; and *hakkebøf* (HAG-guh-boof), or ground beef fried with onions.

KOLDTBORD

Also known as the open table, *koldtbord* (KOLT-board) is a buffet that consists mainly of cold dishes of herring, fish, meat, salad, and cheeses. The food is eaten in a particular order. The herring and fish dishes are eaten first, followed by the salads and cold meats. Next, diners move on to the hot dishes, followed by the desserts. Cheese is the last course.

FAMOUS DANISH COOKIES

Danish butter cookies are popular throughout the world. The cookies are light and crisp and baked to ensure the best aroma and taste possible. Kjeldsens Danish butter cookies, in particular, have achieved worldwide recognition.

SMØRREBRØD

The smørrebrød (*left*), or open-faced sandwich, can be made with many ingredients, is versatile enough to be eaten for three of the four daily meals, and can be found virtually anywhere in Denmark.
(*A Closer Look, page 71*)

Danes love to eat meat. Pork is the most popular meat, while lamb is expensive and therefore considered a delicacy. Meat dishes are often accompanied by potatoes and pickled beets.

Fish makes up a large part of the Danish diet. Smoked and cured fish, such as herring, mackerel, cod, salmon, and eel, are popular. Other favorite dishes include *gravad laks* (GRAH-vuh LAHKS), which is cured or salted salmon marinated in dill and served with a sweet mustard sauce; *kogt torsk* (KOGT TOHSK), or poached cod in mustard sauce; fried plaice; and curried herring.

Danes also have a sweet tooth, and Danish pastries, layered cakes, and sponge cakes with cream fillings are all popular. Favorite cakes include *kringle* (KRING-gluh), or nut-filled coffee cake. *Wienerbrød* (VEE-nuh-brohd) are known internationally as "Danishes." These rich pastries have many sweet fillings, including marzipan, apple purée, and cream.

Danes drink coffee at breakfast, after lunch, and throughout the day during coffee breaks. Aquavit, a strong liqueur flavored with caraway seeds, is a favorite after-dinner drink. Denmark's Carlsberg and Tuborg breweries produce two well-known brands of beer.

DANISH CHEESES

Denmark is acclaimed internationally for its cheeses. The country's most famous cheese is cream Havarti, which is a mild, very creamy, semisoft cheese. When mature, the cheese has a subtle but unique taste. Other popular cheeses include Samso, Danbo, and Esrom.

A CLOSER LOOK AT DENMARK

Denmark is a land of natural beauty. Its landscape ranges from open farmland to forests, from lakes to islands, and from gently rolling hills to sandy beaches. In contrast, self-governing Greenland is covered mostly by ice. Nevertheless, the island is home to a thriving community of Inuit and Danish peoples.

Over the centuries, Denmark has developed and nurtured a prominent arts scene. Eminent thinkers and writers include the philosopher Søren Kierkegaard and author Hans Christian

Below: **With hills that are never too steep to overcome, beautiful and varied countryside, ten national bicycle routes, and 4,350 miles (7,000 km) of marked regional and local routes, Denmark is the ideal destination for a cycling holiday.**

Andersen. The country also boasts the internationally renowned Royal Danish Ballet, fun-packed Legoland, and an annual four-day rock music festival in Roskilde.

An ecologically aware nation, Denmark has done much to protect the environment; the country has actively pursued and developed the use of alternative fuels and now leads the world in the field of wind power.

From the leadership of Valdemar I and subsequent monarchs to the courageous acts of bravery carried out by members of the Danish resistance movement during World War II, Danes have always fought for their beliefs.

Opposite: **A father and daughter enjoy one of the many rides available at BonBon-Land, an amusement park on the island of Zealand.**

Alternative Fuels

Until the 1970s, Denmark was heavily dependent on foreign supplies for energy sources, particularly fossil fuels. The Danish economy was hit hard by the drastic increase in oil prices in the 1970s, and these increases forced the government to rethink its energy strategies. Unlike many other European nations that opted for nuclear power, Denmark turned to wind power.

Wind Power!

The move to wind power made sense for Denmark, which is located in one of the breeziest parts of the world. Windmills, also referred to as wind turbines, were quickly developed to harness the country's prevailing western winds. Windmills in western Jutland were the first to produce energy from wind in 1980.

Windmills are incredibly effective. A single windmill can provide enough electricity for an entire farm, with enough energy left over to sell to a power plant. As a result, wind power has become a big business for Denmark. Today the country dominates

Left: **Large wind turbines have been erected in open fields throughout the Danish countryside, while private windmills can be seen in many backyards. Harnessing wind power does not release carbon dioxide into the atmosphere, which has enabled Denmark to reduce its greenhouse gas emissions.**

the wind power industry. In 2000, the wind industry employed about sixteen thousand people, and wind generated an estimated 13 percent of Denmark's electricity consumption. Danish companies supply over half the windmills used worldwide, and the windmill is now one of the country's largest exports.

The election of Anders Fogh Rasmussen as prime minister, however, may lead to a shift in Denmark's wind-energy policies. The government has proposed to reduce spending on wind-energy research to increase funding for the country's welfare system.

Electric Cars

Danish experiments with electric cars have met with less initial success. An early model of a Danish electric car was the three-wheeled Ellert. Designed for short trips, the car performed best in city traffic. The Ellert, however, carried only the driver and had little space for luggage. In addition, concerns were raised about the car's safety. Consequently, the Ellert did not become a commercial success. Today the government is trying to encourage the use of electric vehicles (EVs) and has set up the Electric Vehicle Information Centre (VCE) to help promote EVs.

Above: **Since electric cars use very little energy and do not contribute to air pollution, they are environmentally friendly modes of transportation.**

THE LARGEST OFFSHORE WIND FARM

Located in shallow waters 1.2 miles (2 km) outside Copenhagen harbor, Middelgrunden Wind Farm is the world's largest offshore wind farm. Stretching a total length of 2 miles (3.2 km), Middelgrunden's twenty wind turbines generate enough electricity to power 3 percent of Copenhagen's energy needs each year.

Hans Christian Andersen

Hans Christian Andersen is the most famous writer in the history of Denmark. His well-loved fairy tales are considered classics of children's literature, and they have made him Denmark's greatest contributor to world literature.

Born in Odense on April 2, 1805, Hans Christian Andersen moved to Copenhagen in 1819 and entered the Royal Theater the following year in the hopes of becoming an actor. On the recommendation of the theater board, he was sent to school and was admitted to the University of Copenhagen in 1828.

His first success as a writer came in 1829 with the publication of *A Walk from Holmen's Canal to the East Point of the Island of Amager in the Years 1828 and 1829*, a fantastic tale that imitated the style of German writer E. T. A. Hoffmann. Although Andersen went on to write a number of plays, he was regarded as a novelist for a long time.

In 1835, Andersen published his first book of fairy tales, *Fairy Tales, Told for Children*, which included the classic *The Princess and the Pea*. Until his death in 1875, Andersen wrote a total of 190 fairy tales. He gave each story its own personal twist, but his tales essentially break down into four categories: folk tales, such as *The Tinder Box*; tales based on his own life, including *The Ugly Duckling*; tales making fun of human faults, such as *The Emperor's New Clothes*; and philosophical tales, such as *The Story of a Mother* (1848) and *The Shadow* (1847).

Many of his fairy tales take place in Denmark, but others use imaginary settings or settings from around the world. Andersen was extremely successful at humanizing plants, animals, and inanimate objects, and the villains of his tales had human weaknesses rather than being imaginary witches or trolls. Andersen's focus was to educate and improve human behavior, as well as to entertain.

Although Andersen continued to write novels, plays, and accounts of his travels until his death, his fairy tales brought him worldwide fame and established him as one of the great figures of world literature.

Above: This illustration shows a scene from *The Steadfast Tin Soldier* (1838). Hans Christian Andersen's fairy tales have been translated into more than 120 languages and have inspired plays, ballets, films, and works of art.

Opposite: This statue of Hans Christian Andersen is located in Copenhagen. During his lifetime, Andersen considered himself an outsider and did not feel that he had been completely accepted by society. He was a sensitive man who sought fame, success, and love, but he only achieved the first two. Andersen wrote *The Ugly Duckling* with the idea that life could change for the better, but he never underwent the sort of metamorphosis that served his lead character so well.

Christmas

Denmark's hearty winters, friendly inhabitants, and creative cuisine combine to make *jul* (YOOL), or Christmas, a very special time. Unlike many other countries that celebrate Christmas on December 24 and 25, Christmas in Denmark is almost a month-long celebration.

The festivities begin on December 1, when families light candles, place wreaths in windows, and put up decorations. Many Danish children have Christmas calendars, sometimes made by a member of the family, that contain twenty-four small gifts so the child can open a little present every morning until Christmas Eve.

In Denmark, food has always played an important role in Christmas celebrations, and families make cookies and sweets together as part of the Christmas preparations. Traditional Christmas cookies include vanilla flavored wreaths; *brune kager* (BROO-nuh KAY-yuh), or gingerbread; *klejner* (KLY-nuh), which

Below: **Christmas in Denmark is a time for families and friends to gather and enjoy the festive season.**

Left: This traditional Christmas dinner consists of roast pork and special seasonal trimmings, including sweet-and-sour red cabbage and caramelized potatoes, with rich, brown gravy.

SAINT LUCIA DAY

On December 13, Saint Lucia Day processions take place throughout the country. On this day, processions of children dressed in white and each carrying a candle visit schools, hospitals, rest homes, and other institutions and sing songs. A young girl wearing a crown of candles on her head leads each procession. Originating in Sweden, this festival gained popularity in Denmark after World War II.

is fried knotted dough; and *pebernødder* (pay-wuh-NOOL-luh), or spiced cookies.

The main Jul celebrations take place on December 24. In the morning, Danish families decorate a Christmas tree with candles, small cones filled with candy, heart-shaped ornaments, and strings of small Danish flags. Christmas dinner is also prepared, and some families attend church services in the afternoon. In the evening, Danes have their traditional Christmas dinner. This dinner includes roast pork or apple-stuffed roast goose or duck, sweet-and-sour red cabbage, liver pâté, and caramelized potatoes. Rice pudding with sugar, cinnamon, and butter is always served as dessert. A whole almond is hidden in the pudding, and whoever gets the almond is said to receive good luck throughout the new year and also receives a present, which is traditionally a marzipan pig. After the meal, families join hands and walk around the Christmas tree, singing Christmas carols and traditional festive songs. They then exchange and open presents.

The celebrations continue on December 25, when Danish households host a lunch for the extended family. Danes also spend this day visiting friends.

CHRISTMAS HEARTS

The Christmas heart, a special Danish tradition, is an interwoven paper heart that is often red and white, the colors of the Danish flag. These hearts are hung on Christmas trees, doors, and windows.

Danish Vikings

Vikings have taken on a mythology all their own, demonized by some and romanticized by others. Vikings were great sailors and regarded as cruel and ferocious enemies, but they were also great storytellers and skilled craftspeople and workers.

At Home

The Vikings had a complex culture, with developed religious traditions, poetry, and art. Most men were farmers who grew barley, rye, oats, and wheat and raised cattle, pigs, horses, and sheep. The women looked after the home; they were also expected to manage the farms when their husbands were away. The Vikings had a system of laws, and they worshiped a number of gods, including Thor and Odin. Many Vikings converted to Christianity in the tenth century and are credited with helping spread the religion throughout Denmark.

RAISING VIKING SHIPS

In the 1950s, five Viking ships were discovered in Roskilde Fjord. The ships had been sunk to close one of the lanes leading into the important commercial town of Roskilde. In 1962, the two cargo ships, two longships, and one ferry, or fishing boat, were raised. Today, the well-preserved remains of the ships are on view at the Viking Ship Museum in Roskilde, alongside another longship that was discovered in 1997.

EUROPEAN CONQUESTS

In 845, Danish king
Horik sent a Danish
fleet into present-
day Germany and
plundered Hamburg. In
the same year, Paris was
devastated, and the city
had to pay a large ransom
to end the Vikings' siege
of the city. Once the
Vikings had a stronghold
in England, the Danes
raided France on a
regular basis. In 911, the
Viking chieftain Rollo
reached an agreement
with King Charles III of
France whereby the
Danes were granted
control of much of the
area in France now
known as Normandy.
In return, these Vikings
vowed to defend the area
against other Vikings.

Legends in Longships

Viking ships have long been the symbol of the Viking era. The
Vikings used two main types of ships — the longship and the cargo
ship. Ranging from 45 to 75 feet (14 to 23 m) in length, the longship
was narrow and had a single square sail, which gave the ship
speed and maneuverability. The cargo ship, on the other hand,
was a sturdy boat designed to carry men, animals, and supplies.

Raids Abroad

Danish Vikings began raiding neighboring countries in the early
800s. They looted and burned towns along the coast of the areas
that now make up Belgium, France, and the Netherlands. In 865,
Danish Vikings invaded England and conquered much of the
country. By 954, however, successive English kings had regained
the conquered lands.

The revival of Viking raids throughout England began in
980 and steadily intensified. Danish king Sweyn exhausted the
English in annual raids by 1013, and his son, Canute (Knud),
became king of England in 1016. Danish rule over England and
the Viking threat ended in 1042, with King Hardecanute's death.

The Danish Welfare State

With the support of high Danish tax rates, the country's government provides extensive social services, including free medical care, hospitalization, and old-age pensions. As a result of this outstanding system, the Danish life expectancy for both men and women is very high.

Security from the Cradle to the Grave

A leading principle of the Danish welfare state is that no citizen should suffer any hardship, and the needy in Denmark receive various forms of help from the government, including cash benefits. All Danish citizens are entitled to health care, free education, unemployment benefits, housing allowances, child support, and much more.

Families enjoy an extensive range of benefits. Besides the twenty-four weeks of parental leave granted after the birth of

Opposite: **The Danish welfare system provides funds for retirement homes to offer exercise programs to residents to help keep them active.**

Below: **Danish children are entitled to free dental care.**

a child, childcare leave for up to twelve months is also available to new parents. A tax-free benefit, known as the children's check, is paid annually to parents with children under the age of eighteen. In addition, childcare services are available for children up to the age of six.

The welfare system provides free education for all children, from elementary school to master's degrees at the university level. The government also subsidizes newspapers, publishing houses, film and music projects, theaters, public libraries, and sports organizations.

Sick leave insurance ensures that unwell employees receive between 80 and 90 percent of their salary, while unemployed people receive income support. A publicly funded old-age pension is available to all citizens over sixty-five years of age.

The government dominates new housing projects. Housing allowances are given to households with little money, and loans with attractive interest rates are given to developers. The elderly are offered services, such as home help with cleaning, to help them manage in their own homes. Otherwise, the state provides specially adapted housing or apartments in retirement homes.

DOES THE DANISH MODEL WORK?

Some Danes, especially those who make a lot of money, have left their homeland to avoid paying what they consider excessive taxes. In addition, complaints have recently been raised about the quality of services and the effectiveness of the government's bureaucracy. Those considerations merit attention, but most Danes are satisfied with the way the welfare system is set up and with the services and security offered by their government.

Denmark and the Holocaust

Concerned about Nazi Germany's expansionist policies, Denmark signed a nonagression treaty with its powerful neighbor in May 1939. When other European nations declared war later that year, Denmark declared its neutrality. Nazi Germany, however, invaded Denmark on April 9, 1940. Hopelessly outmatched, the Danish government was quickly forced to surrender. In turn, the Germans agreed not to interfere in Denmark's internal affairs.

A Resistance Is Born

A resistance movement began to make itself felt in 1941 after the government signed the Anti-Comintern Pact, which prohibited all communist activity. The movement was slow to develop but had gained momentum by mid-1943. In August of that year,

Below: **A group of Danish resistance fighters poses for a photograph on its armored vehicle. The movement's main operations included industrial and railway sabotage to block the movement of German troops. If caught, resistance members faced the death penalty or deportation to a German concentration camp.**

large-scale protests ended all cooperation between the Danish government and the occupying forces. The Germans took control of the country, and the protesting Danes formed the secret Danish Freedom Council to lead the fight for the nation's liberation.

Solving the Jewish Question

In September 1943, Nazi dictator Adolf Hitler authorized the deportation of Denmark's Jews to Germany. German sources, however, leaked a warning about the impending deportation to members of the Danish resistance. The Danes sprang into action, organizing a nationwide effort to smuggle the country's Jewish community to neutral Sweden by sea. They provided Jewish Danes with hiding places, food, and transportation to the coast.

Danish fishermen played a vital role in the rescue operation because they provided the main means of transportation to Sweden. Smuggling Jews was extremely dangerous; the fishermen risked their boats and businesses, as well as imprisonment or deportation to a German concentration camp. Within a two-week period, more than seven thousand Danish Jews had been smuggled to safety in Sweden.

Due to the valiant efforts of the Danish people, the German forces succeeded in capturing only a small portion of Denmark's Jewish community. In total, 481 Danish Jews were deported to the Theresienstadt ghetto in the present-day Czech Republic. All but fifty-one survived the Holocaust.

A NATIONAL SYMBOL

King Christian X became a prominent figure for the Danish population during the years of German occupation. Unlike members of other European royal families who fled to England to lead resistance movements from there, King Christian chose to remain with his people in Denmark. Every morning, the king rode his horse through the streets of Copenhagen, unarmed and without escort, to underline his continuing claims for national sovereignty.

GILLELEJE

The inhabitants of Gilleleje, a village in the northernmost part of Zealand, were instrumental in hiding and transporting Danish Jews to Sweden. One of the safe havens for Jews waiting for transportation was the village's church, which dates back to 1538. In total, about one-fifth of the Danish Jews escaped to Sweden via this village.

Greenland

With a land area of 840,000 square miles (2,175,600 square km), Greenland is the largest island in the world. A dependency of the Kingdom of Denmark, Greenland was granted home rule in 1979 by the Danish Parliament.

Canada's Ellesmere Island lies 16 miles (26 km) to the northwest of Greenland, and the nearest European country is Iceland to the southeast. Two-thirds of Greenland lies within the Arctic Circle. The island's capital and largest city is Nuuk.

Greenland's interior ice-covered plateau covers nearly 85 percent of the island. The island's coastal areas are ice free and indented with fjords. The climate is extremely cold: the average winter temperatures range from 21° F (-6° C) in the south to -31° F (-35° C) in the north. Average summer temperatures in the south are 45° F (7° C) and 39° F (4° C) in the north. Mammals in Greenland include wolves, reindeer, polar bears, and arctic foxes. Various seals, whales, and fish make their homes in the surrounding waters.

Below: **Most of Greenland, such as this village in the central part of the island, is covered by snow all year round. An enterprising Viking named the island Greenland in an unsuccessful effort to attract settlers. In reality, the only part of Greenland that is ever green is the coast, and this area is only green during the island's short summer.**

The island's economy relies mainly on fishing and financial support from the Danish government. The fish catch is primarily cod, shrimp, halibut, and salmon; fish processing is another major industry. Agriculture is only possible on about 1 percent of the land in the southern regions. Farmers raise sheep and reindeer for meat, wool, and milk and grow hay and garden vegetables. An extensive deposit of gold was discovered on Greenland in 1989, but the island's harsh climate and rugged terrain have made subsequent mining extremely difficult.

Above: **Many members of the island's Inuit community promote their cultural identity by wearing the Inuit national costume. The costume consists of an inner tunic, a parka, pants, leggings worn over the pants, sealskin boots, and gloves. Fur and leather patchwork, embroidery, and sometimes beads are used to decorate the clothing.**

The Greenlanders

Eighty-eight percent of the people on Greenland are native Greenlanders. Danes and other ethnic groups make up the remainder of the population. Greenlanders are Inuit or of mixed Inuit and European origin. Greenland's population is widely dispersed, with most living in small settlements dotted along the coast. About one-fourth of the people live in Nuuk, the capital city. Greenlandic, an Inuit language with some Danish words, and Danish are the most common languages.

Søren Kierkegaard

Arguably no man has enjoyed as broad an influence on contemporary thought as Søren Kierkegaard. While generally regarded as the father of existentialism, Kierkegaard's influence reaches far beyond academic circles regarding Christianity, psychology, and literature.

Kierkegaard was born into a wealthy family on May 5, 1813, and attended the University of Copenhagen, where he eventually obtained a master's degree in theology. He was perhaps most influenced by his troubled relationship with his father, Michael Kierkegaard, who was a deeply religious man, and his relationship with Regina Olsen to whom he became engaged.

After calling off the engagement, Kierkegaard wrote *Either/Or: A Fragment of Life* (1843). In this book, Kierkegaard states his belief in the necessity for individuals to make their own conscious and responsible choices among the alternatives that life offers. This belief has since become the basis of all existential writing and thought.

Above: **A statue of Søren Kierkegaard is located outside the Royal Library in Copenhagen.**

Left: **Søren Kierkegaard lived part of his adult life in this building in Copenhagen.**

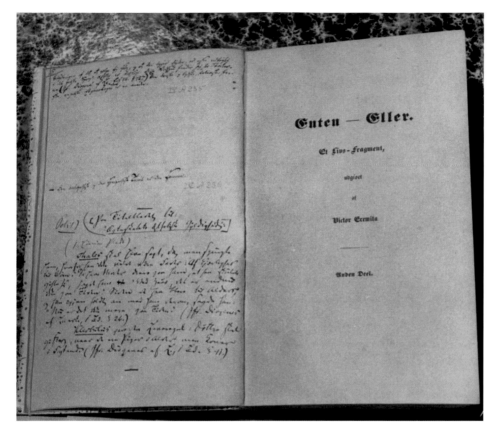

Left: This copy of *Enten-Eller: Et Livs Fragment*, or *Either/Or: A Fragment of Life*, shows handwritten notes jotted down by Søren Kierkegaard. Other influential works of Kierkegaard include *Fear and Trembling* (1843), *Repetition* (1843), and *Stages on Life's Way* (1845).

"THE GREAT EARTHQUAKE"

An event that occurred during Michael Kierkegaard's childhood is believed to have had a profound effect on him and his son Søren. As a child, Michael worked as a helper on a farm in western Jutland. One day, the young Michael cursed God for his hardships and poverty. Soon after, he was sent to live with an uncle in Copenhagen. There, his fortunes changed, and he became a successful businessman. Despite this change in fortune and his refound faith in God, Michael was convinced that his blasphemy had cursed his family, a fact that seemed to be confirmed by the premature deaths of his wife and five of their children. Søren was horrified when he learned of his father's sin and described the traumatic effect of the revelation as "the Great Earthquake."

As a philosopher, Kierkegaard threw himself wholeheartedly into his relationship with God and wrote endlessly on the subject. In the later years of his life, Kierkegaard spent an increasing amount of time criticizing the established Church of Denmark and its clergy. Works written by him during this time include *Works of Love* (1847) and *Training in Christianity* (1850). The conflict with the Church greatly affected Kierkegaard's health, and he died at the age of forty-two on November 11, 1855.

Kierkegaard and Modern Existentialism

Although practically unknown outside Denmark during the nineteenth century, Kierkegaard later had tremendous influence on both contemporary theology and the philosophical movement known as existentialism. Interest in his work first came with the publication of a book on Kierkegaard by Danish literary critic Georg Brandes in 1877. In the years between World War I and World War II, knowledge of his works became widespread, but only after World War II were his writings fully understood and appreciated.

Legoland

A theme park that encourages creativity, play, and development, Legoland awes and delights both children and adults with its amazing miniature replicas of well-known sights, monuments, and personalities, as well as its many hands-on activities. Located in Billund, the famous toy company's amusement park advertises itself as the only place on Earth where visitors are surrounded by more than fifty million Lego bricks.

Legoland is divided into themed areas that are designed to appeal to children of various age groups. MiniLand is a miniature world of various historic and cultural sites made of Lego bricks, such as the Statue of Liberty; castles on the Rhine River; and many Danish scenes including a traditional village, the Amalienborg Royal Palace in Copenhagen, and the port of Copenhagen. Other highlights include Lego pirates and boats in Pirateland, Lego safari animals and a jungle path

TOY OF THE CENTURY

Lego, the traditional toy of budding young architects and builders, was named the toy of the twentieth century by *Forbes* magazine and the British Association of Toy Retailers. The colorful bricks beat the teddy bear and Barbie to win the coveted title. Today, Legos are sold in over 138 countries, and around 300 million children and adults have bought Lego bricks.

in Adventure Land, and Lego castles and a dragon ride for thrill-seeking visitors in Castleland.

For the most part, Legoland is constructed from the standard eight-studded plastic bricks that can be bought in virtually any toy store. On a few occasions, however, Lego designers have had to manufacture special colors for particular models. All the Lego-made models are functional — trains run according to signaling systems, church organs play music, and ships sail.

In addition to the themed areas, Legoland offers several indoor exhibits. The world-renowned Doll Museum contains about four hundred dolls that date back to 1580, as well as fifty dollhouses. The most famous dollhouse in the collection is Titania's Palace, which features eighteen halls filled with three thousand tiny models of inlaid furniture, paintings, sculptures, and linens decorated with gold, silver, and precious stones.

Since the park was opened in 1968, more than thirty million people have visited Legoland. Today, approximately 1.4 million visitors make their way to the amusement park each year, and seven out of ten visitors are adults — one-fifth of whom come without children.

Above: **Duplo Land is designed for younger children. This area also houses the Traffic School where children can learn to drive in Lego cars. The driving course has traffic lights, intersections, and a crossing where a Lego train speeds past.**

Opposite: **With a current area of 1,076,400 square feet (100,000 square m), Legoland was the brainchild of Godtfred Kirk Christiansen, the son of the founder of the Lego empire. Christiansen originally envisaged a small garden that would display various Lego models and figures. When work began, the project grew, and a much-larger Legoland opened in 1968.**

The Monarchy

The Danish monarchy is one of the oldest in the world, dating back more than one thousand years. The monarchy in Denmark has typically been patriarchal — fifty kings and one queen ruled the country prior to 1972. Throughout the centuries, all of these monarchs served as focal points for the Danish population.

The House of Glücksborg, to which the current monarch belongs, became royalty only in 1863. The family, however, is descended in direct male line from the royal house that dates back to King Gorm, who ruled in the tenth century.

Born a week after the Nazi invasion of Denmark, Queen Margrethe's birth on April 16, 1940, was regarded as a welcome distraction by the Danish population. In 1953, the country's constitution was amended to allow females to ascend the throne. As a result, Margrethe assumed the title of "throne heiress" and took her place in the Danish State Council on her eighteenth birthday.

THE FATHER-IN-LAW OF EUROPE

Many Danish monarchs strengthened the state by marrying into the royal families of other nations. Christian IX (r. 1863–1906) was the most notable in this regard. He became known as the "father-in-law of Europe" because his descendants came to occupy the thrones of Denmark, Norway, Great Britain, Greece, and Russia.

Below: Queen Margrethe and Prince Henrik attend a state dinner in Versailles, France, in 1993.

Above (from left to right): **Princess Alexandra, Prince Joachim, Prince Nikolai, Queen Margrethe, and Prince Henrik celebrate the queen's sixtieth birthday on April 16, 2000.**

Margrethe became Queen Margrethe II of Denmark on January 14, 1972, following the death of her father, King Frederik IX. Since then, she has worked hard to bring the royal family into closer contact with the Danish people and, as a result, has helped consolidate the popularity of the royal family.

As head of state, Queen Margrethe II takes part in forming new governments, is formally the head of the government, and represents Denmark abroad. She keeps herself politically informed and is briefed weekly by the prime minister and foreign ministers on issues of state. In addition, the queen's signature is required on all new parliamentary acts.

Apart from her many official and ceremonial functions, Queen Margrethe II is an accomplished linguist and artist. She has translated books from Swedish into Danish and, with her husband Prince Henrik, from French into Danish. As an artist, she has illustrated a 1977 edition of J.R.R. Tolkien's *Lord of the Rings* (1954–1955), as well as designed costumes and scenery for a television production of Hans Christian Andersen's *The Shepherdess and the Chimney Sweep* (1845). One of the queen's greatest works was her set designs for the Royal Danish Ballet's performance in 1991 of *A Folk Tale* (1845).

BEFORE BECOMING QUEEN

After graduating from high school, Margrethe continued her studies at Danish and overseas universities. In 1967, she married Count Henri de Laborde de Monpezat, a French diplomat, who took the title of Prince Henrik. They have two sons, Crown Prince Frederik and Prince Joachim.

Overfishing

Denmark's geographic location makes it ideal for fishing, with the North Sea, the Baltic Sea, the Skagerrak, and the Kattegat surrounding much of the country. These waters have always been well stocked with numerous species of fish, including cod, plaice, mackerel, and herring. An increasing population and improvements in technology, however, have led the Danes to almost fish themselves out of business.

A Formula for Disaster

Despite its relatively small size, Denmark is among the world's top fishing nations. This status is due mainly to technological advancements, including the development of steam and diesel engines and sonar, that have made fishing easier and more efficient. These improvements, however, have made fishing more and more intensive over the years. As a result, increased fishing served to decrease the fish populations in Danish waters to the extent that both the survival of particular fish species and the livelihood of Danish fishers were threatened.

Below: For centuries, fishers have beached their boats along the west coast of Jutland. Denmark's largest fishing port, Esbjerg, is located in eastern Ribe on the North Sea. The many species of fish that make their home in the North Sea are of great economic importance to Danish fishers.

What Is Being Done?

The problem of overfishing became apparent at the beginning of the 1980s. During the mid-1980s, therefore, the government held a series of "TAC," or "total allowable catches," meetings. Quotas were put in place, and measures were taken to revive the dwindling fish populations. Further steps were taken in the early 1990s, when the government financially supported a reduction in the fishing fleet to alleviate structural problems in the industry. This action led to the number of fishers being halved.

Today, the European Union engages in an annual review of fish populations and allots fishing quotas to all member nations. Now, Danish fishers catch nearly 2 million tons (1,814,400 metric tonnes) of fish each year, 80 percent of which come from the North Sea and the Skagerrak. Although these fishing quotas are hotly debated by Danish and other European fishers, Denmark continues to be one of the world's leading seafood exporters.

Above: **This woman proudly displays a cod she caught in the North Sea. Apart from industrial fishing and fishing for human consumption, fishing is also a popular pastime, and many charter boats offer enthusiasts the opportunity to fish in Danish waters.**

Roskilde Festival

For four days each summer, the Roskilde Festival rocks Denmark. Held during either the last weekend in June or the first weekend in July, the festival is the largest of its kind in Europe. The first festival took place in 1971, and the event has grown continuously since then. Now more than 150 artists and bands perform on seven stages during the festival.

The Early Years

During the late 1960s, young adults began to turn to large, days-long, outdoor music events for relaxation. The most famous of these festivals was the Woodstock Festival that was first held in the United States in 1969. The festival trend hit Denmark in 1971, when large festivals were held in Randers, Nyborg, and Hillerød. The final and biggest music festival of the year, however, was the festival that took place near Roskilde. Although poorly organized, the festival featured around twenty bands and attracted a crowd of about ten thousand each day.

During the 1970s, the Roskilde Festival evolved. Organization improved when the *Foreningen Roskildefonden* (The Roskilde Charity Society) began to manage the festival, and the festival volunteers began to gain experience. The number of people

Left: **Many performances take place simultaneously on different stages at Roskilde Festival. Here, crowds gather at the Orange Stage to listen to popular bands perform. Around seventy thousand people attend the festival each year, and all the profits from the festival are donated to humanitarian projects and charities.**

Left: **The legendary Bob Dylan performed on the Orange Stage at Roskilde Festival in 2001.**

attending the event grew each year, and the quality of both service facilities and music programs steadily improved. In 1978, the organizers of the event bought the Orange Stage, and the stage has been the festival's famous symbol ever since. In the same year, the festival organizers began to get world-class acts to headline a program characterized by new and young bands.

A World-Class Festival

Today, the Roskilde Festival is one of the best-run, largest, and most-prestigious contemporary music festivals in the world. Internationally renowned acts, including Robbie Williams, Bob Dylan, Lou Reed, and U2, are scheduled to perform each year. Music lovers come from nearby nations, such as Germany, Sweden, Finland, Norway, and the Netherlands, and from as far away as Japan and the United States.

Royal Danish Ballet

The Royal Danish Ballet was founded in 1748 as the dance element of the Royal Theater. Today, the centuries-old Royal Danish Ballet enjoys international acclaim and is world famous for its classical style of ballet.

Three Great Ballet Masters

In 1775, Italian Vincenzo Galeotti (1733–1816) became the director of the Royal Danish Ballet. Through his work, Galeotti introduced the *ballet d'action*, in which the plot is expressed in dance and pantomime. He also created dramatic works inspired by literature, basing ballets on the works of Shakespeare and Voltaire. One of his works, *The Whims of Cupid and the Ballet Master* (1786), is the world's oldest ballet to retain its original choreography.

In the mid-nineteenth century, the Royal Danish Ballet took its present form under the leadership of choreographer and ballet master August Bournonville (1805–1879). Under Bournonville, the ballet company entered a period of greatness.

Below: **Located in Copenhagen, the Royal Theater houses the national theater, ballet, and opera companies.**

Above: **These ballerinas are performing in the ballet** *Tornerose.*

For almost fifty years, he perfected the ballet and encouraged original Danish contributions to the international ballet repertoire by developing the Danish style of classical ballet. All his ballets included parts that enabled him to demonstrate his skillfulness as a dancer, and these ballets later established and displayed the excellence of Danish male dancing.

After a period of decline, the Royal Danish Ballet was revived by Harald Lander (1905–1971). As artistic director from 1932 to 1951, Lander enriched the company's repertoire. For the first time, Danish ballet gained international recognition, and the company made its first overseas tours.

Elegance in Motion

Throughout the years, the Royal Danish Ballet has developed internationally acclaimed ballerinas, such as Margot Lander (1910–1961) and Toni Lander (1931–1985), and male dancers, such as Erik Bruhn (1928–1986) and Peter Martins (1946–). Today, the Royal Danish Ballet has a troupe of nearly one hundred dancers.

DENMARK'S PRIMA BALLERINA

Born in Copenhagen in 1910, Margot Lander joined the Royal Danish Ballet in 1925. She became the company's solo dancer in 1931 and was appointed a prima ballerina in 1942. Lander was especially admired for her portrayal of Swanilda in the ballet *Coppélia* (1870).

Smørrebrød

Probably the most outstanding and most popular of Danish gourmet foods is the smørrebrød, an open-faced sandwich. *Smørrebrød* means "butter and bread," and it forms an integral part of Danish cuisine. While many Danes eat smørrebrød for lunch, this sandwich is also popular for breakfast and as a late evening snack. This famous specialty can be found almost anywhere in Denmark, from the grandest restaurants and exclusive smørrebrød shops to bakeries and street stalls.

Above: A smørrebrød is made up of elaborate layers of wonderful and varied ingredients, and the combinations are endless. The open-faced sandwich often typifies the Danish approach to eating, which is functional yet elegant.

Food as Art

Although a smørrebrød is essentially an open-faced sandwich with one or more toppings, creating it is considered nothing less than an art form. Each sandwich is carefully prepared following centuries-old traditions.

Smørrebrød requires thinly sliced bread with a crisp crust. Although several types of bread can be used, dark rye bread is the most popular. A layer of butter is evenly spread over the bread, and it is important not to miss the edges. The butter stops the bread from becoming soggy and helps keep the toppings in place. Toppings are then placed on the bread, layer upon layer. It is essential that the toppings are not mixed and that no bread is left exposed.

The best-known toppings for a smørrebrød include shrimp, smoked salmon, marinated herring, smoked herring and egg yolk, smoked eel with scrambled eggs, pork with red cabbage, and liver paste with pickled cucumber or gherkins. Practically all kinds of food, however, can be used: cold ham with a fried egg, roast beef with tartar sauce and fried onions, meatloaf with cucumber salad, or cold sausages with scrambled eggs. Popular garnishes include cheese; cucumbers; tomatoes; radishes; caviar; green, yellow, and red peppers; pickles; lettuce; and citrus fruits.

Smørrebrød Etiquette

No matter how elaborate or simple a smørrebrød is, diners must always eat the open-faced sandwich with a knife and fork. In addition, only one smørrebrød at a time should be placed on a plate and consumed.

Opposite: This chef proudly displays a mouthwatering array of smørrebrød. Smørrebrød enthusiasts put a great deal of emphasis on presentation. A smørrebrød must appear attractive before it is proven delicious. A significant part of the smørrebrød experience is to admire your smørrebrød before consuming it.

Valdemar I

Valdemar I was king of Denmark from 1157 until his death in 1182. He is credited with consolidating power within Denmark, ending the Wendish threat to Danish shipping, and winning independence from the Holy Roman Empire.

Born in 1131, Valdemar was a great-grandson of the Danish king Sweyn II. Valdemar's accession to the throne ended twenty-five years of internal fighting and marked the beginning of an era during which the power of the Danish crown was strengthened and Danish territory expanded.

Once in power, Valdemar turned his attention to the attacks on Danish shipping in the Baltic Sea and on the Danish coast by the Wends, or Slavs, who inhabited an area in eastern Germany. When the Wends expanded their territories eastward along the Baltic coastline, Valdemar joined forces with the Saxon prince

Opposite: **During Valdemar's reign, schools, fortresses, monasteries, and churches, such as Bjernede Church on the island of Zealand, were established throughout the country.**

Left: **A skilled statesman, Absalon was King Valdemar's closest adviser. He was also named bishop of Roskilde in 1158.**

Henry II to fight against them. With the support of the Danish church, Valdemar began a series of attacks on the Wends. In 1169, Valdemar's troops captured the Wendish stronghold of Rügen (now in Germany) and their sanctuary at Arcona, subsequently ending the Wendish threat.

During the early years of Valdemar's reign, relations with the German king and Holy Roman emperor Frederick I were turbulent. Valdemar acknowledged Frederick I as his overlord and accepted his antipope Victor IV. This move, however, was unpopular in some circles, and Eskil, Denmark's archbishop of Lund (now in present-day Sweden), fled to France rather than oppose Pope Alexander III. After some deliberation, Valdemar and Bishop Absalon changed their minds and acknowledged Alexander as pope in c. 1165. As a result, Eskil returned to Denmark and confirmed the canonization of Valdemar's father. In addition, Valdemar's son Canute IV was crowned joint king in 1170 by Eskil, ensuring the hereditary rule of the Valdemars and invalidating the overlordship of Frederick I.

THE CLOSING YEARS

Valdemar closed his reign by strengthening Danish defenses against a possible German attack. After ensuring Denmark's defense, he allied himself with Frederick I, this time as almost equal partners. The alliance between the two kings was further strengthened with the marriage of Valdemar's daughter to one of Frederick's sons.

RELATIONS WITH NORTH AMERICA

Ties between Denmark and North America have always been close. In the nineteenth and twentieth centuries, many Danes emigrated to North America in pursuit of a better life. The contribution that these Danish immigrants made to the building of the United States and Canada into the countries they are today has been one of the pillars of Danish-North American relations.

Today, North America has many Danish organizations that are dedicated to preserving and promoting Danish culture. Trade links between the three nations flourish, while political

Opposite: **A miniature version of the Statue of Liberty stands proudly in MiniLand in Legoland, Denmark's world-famous, family-oriented theme park.**

relations are strong. All three countries are dedicated to promoting international peace and stability, and Danish, Canadian, and U.S. troops often participate in peacekeeping missions in war-torn areas of the world.

In recent years, North Americans of Danish descent have taken great interest in learning about their family ties with Denmark, and many travel to Denmark to discover their roots. Danish-North Americans also take pride in their heritage and have established numerous museums, cultural parks, and villages that pay homage to their "old" homeland.

Above: **Popular North American fast-food chains can be found all over Denmark.**

Historical Relations with North America

Relations with North America developed in the nineteenth century. Denmark recognized the United States as a free and independent nation shortly after the U.S. Declaration of Independence, making Denmark the country with which the United States has maintained the longest uninterrupted diplomatic relations. This move opened the way for trading links between the two nations. Denmark's prevailing policy of neutrality after the Franco-German War (1870–1871), however, eliminated any possible military links with North America for many years.

During World War II, Denmark was occupied by German forces for five years. Since the end of the war, Denmark, the United States, and Canada have shared the common goal of maintaining international peace and stability. Denmark and the United States were actively involved in the establishment of the United Nations (U.N.) in 1945, and Canada joined the organization shortly afterward. The three nations were also among the founding members of the North Atlantic Treaty Organization (NATO) in 1949.

Below: **Danish Count Reventlow (***fourth from left***), American General Dwight D. Eisenhower (***eighth from left***), and Canadian L.D. Wilgress (***first from right***) attend a NATO meeting in London in 1951.**

Although relations between the three countries have remained strong, Denmark and the United States have had differences of opinion on a number of issues. Denmark was critical of the U.S. war policy in Vietnam during the late 1960s and early 1970s. In the 1980s, further conflict arose between the United States and Denmark regarding nuclear weapons and arms control issues. Since the end of the Cold War, however, Denmark has been actively supportive of U.S. security policies in NATO and acknowledges the importance of both the United States and Canada continuing to be active participants in the organization.

Above: **U.S. president Bill Clinton (***right***) waves to a crowd of onlookers during his visit to Denmark in 1997.**

Arctic Ties

Canada's Arctic boundary with Greenland has led to extensive interaction and cooperation with Denmark over the years. Canada, Denmark, and Greenland have participated in various international commissions dealing with conservation, tourism, and scientific research. In addition, Denmark, Canada, and the United States all joined the Arctic Council in 1996. The Council focuses on the Arctic's environment and ways to improve the economic, social, and cultural well-being of the Arctic nations.

THULE AIR BASE

With the emergence of the Cold War between the United States and the former Soviet Union after World War II, Denmark allowed the U.S. government to set up an air base in Thule, Greenland. Built in 1951, the base provided a refueling point for long-range bombers potentially directed at the Soviet Union. Thule Air Base and its facilities were home to ten thousand people, including U.S. armed forces, during the years of the Cold War.

Immigration

Danish emigration to North America began in the nineteenth century. It was only after 1840, however, that Danes began to arrive in North America in large numbers. Danish Baptists and Mormons left their homeland and settled in Utah, Arizona, and Wisconsin. These immigrants were soon followed by both rural and urban Danes. By the mid-nineteenth century, emigration to North America was an attractive alternative to the harsh life Danes faced in Denmark as an increase in the Danish population brought about difficult working and living conditions.

Approximately twenty thousand Danes emigrated to the United States between 1870 and 1895. Many of these immigrants established settlements in Nebraska, Iowa, Kansas, North Dakota, South Dakota, Michigan, Minnesota, and California. A further fifty thousand Danes moved to the United States between 1910 and 1930. By this time, Danes had begun to move away from rural areas and farming and had started to settle in U.S. cities,

THE FIRST SETTLERS

The first wave of Danes emigrated to the United States in 1820. As travel costs were expensive, emigration was limited to those who could afford it, such as teachers, tradesmen, and preachers.

Below: An extended Danish family poses for a photograph while waiting to emigrate to Canada in 1957.

Left: **Two Danish women seeking a new life in the United States arrive in New York in the mid-1920s.**

including New York and Chicago. After 1930, Danish emigration continued but on a more modest scale.

Emigration to Canada began in the late nineteenth century, with most Danes choosing to settle in maritime provinces. As the shift from rural to urban living took place in the early twentieth century, Danish laborers, businesspeople, and traders began to move to Canada's major cities. Today, Danish communities can be found in Alberta, British Columbia, New Brunswick, Nova Scotia, and Ontario.

Settling In

Unlike other Scandinavian immigrants, Danes joined U.S. and Canadian churches and left Danish churches in North America struggling to maintain unity and a sense of "Danishness" among immigrants. In addition, Danish immigrants were more likely than their Scandinavian neighbors to spread out geographically rather than settle in one area, thus assimilating quickly into their new surroundings.

Left: Queen Margrethe II of Denmark and President Bill Clinton attend a state dinner in Copenhagen in 2000. Denmark and North America have an active exchange of official visitors and regular high-level government meetings. Art Eggleton, Canada's minister of national defense, visited Copenhagen in February 2001.

Current Relations

Relations between Denmark, the United States, and Canada are excellent. All three countries work closely together in many fields, including human rights and security, democratic development, and combating global terrorism.

Trade ties between the three nations are strong. The United States is Denmark's strongest non-European trade partner, while Canadian-Danish trade is continuously expanding. Denmark's role in European environmental and agricultural issues and its strategic location at the entrance to the Baltic Sea have made Copenhagen a center for North American businesses dealing with the Nordic/Baltic region. Denmark's environmentalists, however, have been critical of President George W. Bush's refusal to comply with the Kyoto Treaty, which aims to curb global warming.

All three countries are active supporters of international peacekeeping. Danish, Canadian, and U.S. troops were part of the U.N. Protection Force (UNPROFOR) that went to Bosnia and Herzegovina, as well as other republics of the former Yugoslavia, between 1992 and 1995 to monitor the restoration of peace and authority in the war-torn area. Today, troops from all three nations continue to serve side by side in Bosnia.

RELATIONS WITH GREENLAND

The U.S. Air Force (USAF) base and early warning radar at Thule, Greenland, serve as an important link in Western defenses, and the United States and Denmark work closely on matters related to the base. In 1994, Denmark and the United States agreed to allow Thule Air Base to be used for limited tourist transit to assist Greenland's economic development.

Canada has warm relations with its close neighbor Greenland. Canada's Inuit community and most Greenlanders share a common culture, language, and traditions, all of which have helped enhance cooperation for greater trade and commercial relations between the two nations. In addition, Greenland has backed Canada in its efforts to preserve the Atlantic fisheries and actively supports the Arctic Council.

North Americans in Denmark

A small number of North Americans make their homes in Denmark. Most North American visitors to the country are of Danish descent, and they often return to their native homeland to visit family and friends or learn more about their ancestry. In addition to hereditary ties, tourism is another reason why North Americans travel and stay in Denmark. Popular attractions include the sights and sounds of Copenhagen, Odense, and the nation's beautiful countryside.

Denmark is also a popular place to study. Most of the country's universities have active student exchange programs that receive North American students. Participating universities include those at Copenhagen and Århus.

The United States and Canada both have embassies in Copenhagen. In addition, both a Danish Canadian and a Danish American Chamber of Commerce operate in Denmark. These chambers serve the Danish-North American business communities and enhance business ties and trade between Denmark and North America.

JAZZ

Originating in New Orleans in the United States, jazz music is very popular in Denmark. In the 1960s, American jazz greats, including Miles Davis and Duke Ellington, often performed in Denmark. In addition, Danish-American Kai Winding (1922–1989) is generally regarded as one of the great jazz trombonists. Today, both New York and Copenhagen boast jazz scenes that are among the liveliest in the world.

Below: North Americans tour the grounds of one of Denmark's beautiful castles.

Danes in North America

North America's Danish population plays an active role in promoting and nurturing its heritage. Most large North American cities have shops that sell Danish goods, as well as Danish delicatessens and restaurants. Many organizations, such as the Dania Society of Chicago, also foster the exchange of culture between the Danish and North American communities.

Danish communities in North America continue to celebrate their Danish roots. Each year, the Tivoli Fest and Jule Fest are held in Elk Horn, Iowa. In addition, the Danish Immigrant Museum in Elk Horn displays exhibits that tell the stories of Danish immigrants. The museum also has a research center that lists the lineage of many Danes who emigrated to the United States.

Several Danish-North American newspapers exist, including *Den Danske Pioneer*, which is widely available throughout the United States. Many American and Canadian universities, such as the University of Oregon and the University of Toronto, offer Scandinavian studies.

THE AMERICAN-SCANDINAVIAN FOUNDATION

The American-Scandinavian Foundation promotes educational and cultural exchanges between the United States, Denmark, and other Scandinavian nations. Based in New York, the foundation offers fellowships, trainee placements, grants, and cultural activities for its members.

Danish Theme Parks, Villages, and Windmills

Mixing education, adventure, and fun, Legoland California was opened in March 1999. A 128-acre (52-hectare) park, Legoland California's six themed areas feature forty interactive attractions, rides, shows, and restaurants. Approximately thirty million Lego bricks were used to create the five thousand models that decorate the interior of the park.

Historically known as the "Danish Capital of America," Solvang is an extensive Danish-themed town located north of Los Angeles. Originally founded by Danish educators in 1911, the town offers authentic Danish architecture, including farmhouses with artificial storks peeping down from the chimneys, as well as a replica of Copenhagen's *Little Mermaid* statue, two museums, an outdoor theater, and hundreds of shops selling Danish goods.

The only authentic working Danish windmill in the United States is found in Elk Horn, Iowa. Originally built to grind grain in the county of Vejle in 1848, the windmill was dismantled and shipped to the United States in 1975. Volunteers rebuilt the windmill piece by piece, and it now serves as the centerpiece of the largest Danish rural settlement in the United States.

Celebrating American Independence Day in Denmark

In 1912, American citizens of Danish descent bought land in Denmark to establish Rebild National Park. They then donated the park to the Danish government with the understanding that American Independence Day would be celebrated on the grounds of the park each year on July 4. This festival continues to be celebrated today and further strengthens the ties of friendship between the United States and Denmark.

Over the years, hundreds of thousands of Danes and Danish-Americans have joined to celebrate the event. Festivities include music, entertainment, and community singing. In addition, prominent Americans and Danes make speeches to the crowds who descend on the park. Well-known speakers include former American presidents George Bush, Ronald Reagan, Jimmy Carter, and Richard Nixon, as well as Queen Margrethe II, who is a frequent participant in the celebrations.

Left: **This Danish woman participates in celebrations that take place in Rebild National Park every July to mark American Independence Day.**

Famous Danes in North America

Born in the United States to Danish parents, John Gutzon de la Mothe Borglum (1867–1941) was a renowned sculptor. He was responsible for the sculpture of Mount Rushmore National Memorial in South Dakota, which features the faces of American presidents George Washington, Thomas Jefferson, Theodore Roosevelt, and Abraham Lincoln and measures 60 feet (18 m) in height.

Rock star Lars Ulrich, the drummer for Metallica, is Danish. Son of Torben Ulrich, the Danish tennis player, Lars Ulrich formed Metallica with his best friend James Hetfield in 1981, after moving to the United States with his parents. The band has gone on to become one of the most popular and influential hard rock bands of the last twenty years, selling around eighty million albums worldwide and winning numerous music awards.

Danish-American Victor Borge was a humorist, an entertainer, and a first-class pianist. Born in Copenhagen, Borge moved to the United States during World War II. He graced the stage for over seventy years and became one of the highest paid entertainers in the United States. Borge was knighted by King Frederik of Denmark and was honored by both the U.S. Congress and the United Nations.

DANISH STARS AND HOLLYWOOD

Talented Danish actors and directors have made a lasting impression on Hollywood. *Babette's Feast*, directed by Dane Gabriel Axel, won the Academy Award for Best Foreign Film in 1987, as did *Pelle the Conqueror* in 1988, which was directed by Dane Bille August. Both films were based on books by renowned Danish authors. August also directed *Smilla's Sense of Snow* (1997), a film based on a novel by Danish author Peter Høeg, which starred Julia Ormond and Gabriel Byrne, as well as Victor Hugo's immortal *Les Miserables* (1998). Well-known Danish actresses include Connie Nielsen, who co-starred in *Gladiator* (2000) with Russell Crowe, and Iben Hjejle, who made her Hollywood debut as the lead actress in the romantic comedy *High Fidelity* (2000).

DENMARK

Ellesmere
Island

• Thule

NORTH
ATLANTIC
OCEAN

Greenland

NUUK ■

Arctic Circle

Faroe
Islands

SWEDEN

N

Skagerrak

• Skagen

Limfjord

• Ålborg

NORDJYLLAND

Kattegat

Rebild
National Park

← Randers Fjord

VIBORG

Randers •

Gudenå

ÅRHUS

Jutland

Øresund

Gilleleje •

RINGKØBING

Lake
Arresø

• Helsingør

Roskilde

Hillerød •

FREDERIKSBORG

Århus •

Yding Skovhøj
(568 ft/173 m) ▲

Billund •

Jelling •

København •

Lund •

KØBENHAVN

RIBE

VEJLE

■ COPENHAGEN

• Esbjerg

Roskilde •

Malmö •

Zealand

Ribe •

Odense •

VESTSJÆLLAND

ROSKILDE

NORTH
SEA

Funen

Nyborg •

FYN

BORNHOL

STORSTRØM

Bor•

SØNDERJYLLAND

Møn

BALTIC

Ærø

SEA

Langeland

Falster

Lolland

G E R M A N Y

Above: Located on Funen Island, Egeskov Castle is the best-preserved Renaissance castle in Europe.

Ærø Island B4–B5
Ålborg B2
Århus (city) B3
Århus (county) A3–B4

Baltic Sea D3–D5
Billund A4
Bornholm (county) D4
Bornholm Island D4

Copenhagen C4

Ellesmere Island B1
Esbjerg A4

Falster Island C5
Faroe Islands A1–A2
Frederiksborg (county)
   C3–C4
Funen Island B4
Fyn (county) B4–B5

Germany A5–D5
Gilleleje C3
Greenland B1–B2
Gudenå River B3–A4

Helsingør C3

Hillerød C4

Jelling A4
Jutland (region) A2–B4

Kattegat B2–C3
København (county) C4

Lake Arresø C4
Langeland Island B4–B5
Limfjord A3–B3
Lolland Island B5–C5
Lund C4

Malmö C4
Møn Island C4–C5

Nordjylland (county)
   A2–B3
North Atlantic Ocean
   B1–B2
North Sea A3–A5
Nuuk B1
Nyborg B4

Odense B4
Øresund C3–C4

Randers B3

Randers Fjord B3
Rebild National
   Park B3
Ribe (city) A4
Ribe (county) A4
Ringkøbing (county)
   A3–A4
Roskilde (city) C4
Roskilde (county) C4
Roskilde Fjord C4

Skagen B2
Skagerrak A2
Sønderjylland (county)
   A4–B5

Storstrøm (county)
   B5–C4
Sweden B1–D4

Thule B1

Vejle (county) A3–B4
Vestsjælland (county)
   B4–C4
Viborg (county) A2–B3

Yding Skovhøj B3

Zealand Island B4–C4

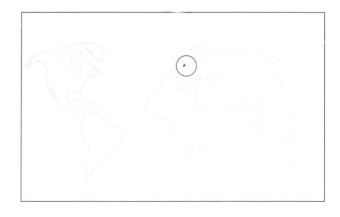

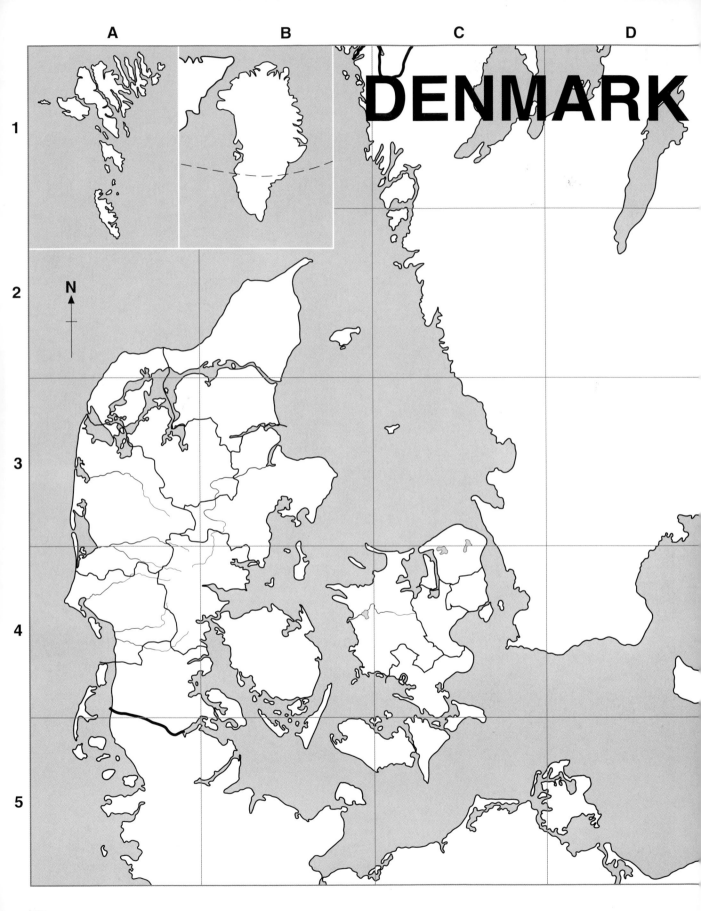

DENMARK

N

A   B   C   D

1

2

3

4

5

88

How Is Your Geography?

Learning to identify the main geographical areas and points of a country can be challenging. Although it may seem difficult at first to memorize the locations and spellings of major cities or the names of mountain ranges, rivers, deserts, lakes, and other prominent physical features, the end result of this effort can be very rewarding. Places you previously did not know existed will suddenly come to life when referred to in world news, whether in newspapers, television reports, other books and reference sources, or on the Internet. This knowledge will make you feel a bit closer to the rest of the world, with its fascinating variety of cultures and physical geography.

Used in a classroom setting, the instructor can make duplicates of this map using a copy machine. (PLEASE DO NOT WRITE IN THIS BOOK!) Students can then fill in any requested information on their individual map copies. Used one-on-one, the student can also make copies of the map on a copy machine and use them as a study tool. The student can practice identifying place names and geographical features on his or her own.

Below: **Poplar trees are a common sight on Funen Island.**

Denmark at a Glance

Official Name	Kingdom of Denmark
Capital	Copenhagen
Main Languages	Danish, Faroese, Greenlandic
Population	5,352,815 (July 2001 estimate)
Land Area	16,639 square miles (43,094 square km)

Note: This figure includes the island of Bornholm, Jutland, and the major islands of Zealand and Funen but excludes the Faroe Islands and Greenland.

Counties	Århus, Bornholm, Frederiksborg, Fyn, København, Nordjylland, Ribe, Ringkøbing, Roskilde, Sønderjylland, Storstrøm, Vejle, Vestsjælland, Viborg
Highest Point	Yding Skovhøj 568 feet (173 m)
Major River	Gudenå
Major Lake	Lake Aresø
Main Religion	Evangelical Lutheranism
Major Cities	Ålborg, Århus, Copenhagen, Odense, Roskilde
Major Holidays	Easter (March/April)
	Liberation Day (May 5)
	Constitution Day (June 5)
	Christmas (December 25)
Major Exports	Chemicals, dairy products, fish, furniture, machinery and instruments, meat and meat products, ships, windmills
Major Imports	Chemicals, consumer goods, grain and foodstuffs, machinery and equipment, raw materials
Currency	Krone (8.62 Kr = U.S. $1 as of 2002)

Opposite: **Tours along Copenhagen's harbor and canals are a popular way to see the sights and sounds of the country's capital city.**

Glossary

Danish Vocabulary

brune kager (BROO-nuh KAY-yuh): gingerbread.

Dannebrog (DAY-nuh-broo): "Danish cloth"; the Danish flag.

Fastelavn (fes-tuh-LAH-on): the Monday before Ash Wednesday.

flæskesteg (FLIE-skuh-tig): roast pork with crackling.

fodbold (FULL-buhn): soccer.

folkeskole (FULL-guh-skool): compulsory elementary and middle school.

Folketing (FULL-guh-ting): the Danish parliament.

frikadeller (FREY-guh-DIL-luh): meatballs.

gravad laks (GRAH-vuh LAHKS): cured or salted salmon marinated in dill and served with a sweet mustard sauce.

gymnasium (gim-NAY-shee-yoom): high school.

hakkebøf (HAG-guh-boof): ground beef with fried onions.

hygge (HOO-guh): "cozy and snug"; the Danish concept that suggests shutting out the trials and tribulations of the outside world and opting for personal warmth and intimacy.

jul (YOOL): Christmas.

klejner (KLY-nuh): fried knotted dough.

kogt torsk (KOGT TOHSK): poached cod in mustard sauce.

koldtbord (KOLT-board): open table; a buffet that consists of cold dishes of fish, meat, salad, and cheese.

kringle (KRING-gluh): a nut-filled coffee cake.

morgenbrød (MWARN-brohd): "morning breads"; breads and rolls that are served at breakfast.

pebernødder (pay-wuh-NOOL-luh): spiced cookies.

smørrebrød (SMUHR-brohd): "butter and bread"; an open-faced sandwich.

wienerbrød (VEE-nuh-brohd): "Viennese bread"; the rich pastries known internationally as "Danishes."

English Words

antipope: a person who is elected or claims to be pope in opposition to another who has been chosen by the church.

bard: a person who composes and recites poems, while playing the harp or lyre.

beached: hauled onto or landed on a beach.

bicameral: consisting of two legislative chambers or houses.

bureaucracy: a system of administrative officials, each dealing with a certain department, under a chief official.

caliber: degree of competence or quality.

canonization: the official declaration of a deceased person as a saint.

charter: an arrangement by which all or part of a ship, airplane, etc., is leased to a group for a particular journey.

choreography: the movements, steps, and patterns that make up a dance.

concentration camp: a military compound used to confine and persecute prisoners.

cooperatives: jointly owned businesses operated by the owners, with profits being shared by the owners.

crackling: the crisp, brown skin of roast pork.

culminated: resulted in; led to.

deportation: expulsion from an area or country.

dioceses: church districts under the jurisdiction of bishops.

existentialism: a philosophical movement that stresses the individual's position as a self-determining agent responsible for his or her own choices.

expansionist: related to a country's policy of increasing its land or power.

fervor: great warmth and earnestness of feeling; passion; zeal.

fjord: a narrow inlet of the sea.

genres: kinds; sorts; styles.

ghetto: a section of a city inhabited predominantly by members of a minority group, usually because of economic or social restrictions.

harnessing: bringing under conditions for effective use; gaining control of for a particular end.

home rule: self-government in local affairs by a city, province, state, or colony.

homogeneous: composed of parts or elements that are similar or the same.

inanimate: not animate; lifeless.

indigenous: originating in or characteristic of a particular region or country.

lobby: try to influence legislation or administrative decisions.

metamorphosis: a complete change in appearance, character, or circumstances.

overlord: a person who is lord over other lords and consequently has great influence or power.

pagan: related to a religion that worships more than one god.

patriarchal: relating to the male head of a family or tribal line.

prodigies: people, especially children or young people, who have extraordinary talent or ability.

pseudonym: a fictitious name used by an author to hide his or her identity.

rearmament: the process of building up a new stock of military weapons.

Reformation: a religious movement that resulted in the formation of new Protestant religions throughout Europe during the sixteenth century.

romanticism: the eighteenth- and nineteenth-century movement in literature and art that was concerned with the expression of the individual's feelings and emotions.

sabotage: destruction of property or obstruction of public services, in order to undermine a government or military effort.

satire: a literary composition in which human folly and vice are scorned and ridiculed.

secular: not relating to religion.

siege: the act of surrounding and attacking a fortified place in such a way as to compel the surrender of its defenders.

sovereign: ruler; monarch.

subsidize: aid a private business with public money.

unicameral: consisting of a single legislative chamber or house.

vested: placed or settled in the possession or control of someone.

More Books to Read

Andersen's Fairy Tales. Wordsworth Children's Classics. Hans Christian Andersen (NTC Publishing Group)

Darkness over Denmark: The Danish Resistance and the Rescue of the Jews. Ellen Levine (Holiday House)

Denmark. Enchantment of the World series. Martin Hintz (Children's Press)

Denmark. Major World Nations series. Alan James (Chelsea House)

Denmark: City and Village Life. Country Insights series. Ole Steen Hansen (Raintree/Steck-Vaughn)

Greenland Mummies. Time Travelers series. Janet Buell (Millbrook Press)

Number the Stars. Lois Lowry (Bantam Doubleday Dell)

Tycho Brahe: Astronomer. Great Minds of Science series. Mary Gow (Enslow)

The Viking News. History News series. Rachel Wright (Gareth Stevens)

Videos

Royal Families of the World: Monaco, Spain, Denmark, Luxembourg, The Habsburgs. (Goldhil Home Media)

Travel the World: Scandinavia — Denmark, Sweden, and Norway. (Questar)

Video Visits: Denmark — The Jewel of Europe. (IVN Entertainment)

The Vikings. (NOVA)

Web Sites

www.andersen.sdu.dk/index_e.html

www.denmark.org/home/index.shtml

www.denmarkemb.org

www.greenland-guide.dk/default.htm

Due to the dynamic nature of the Internet, some web sites stay current longer than others. To find additional web sites, use a reliable search engine with one or more of the following keywords to help you locate information about Denmark. Keywords: *Hans Christian Andersen, Copenhagen, Legoland, Royal Danish Ballet,* smørrebrød.

Index